The Funeral and Wedding

HANDBOOK

The Funeral and Wedding

HANDBOOK

ROBERT BLAIR

CSS Publishing Company, Inc., Lima, Ohio

Second Edition
Copyright © 2001
CSS Publishing Company, Inc.

Cover Design by Daryl Williams

Drawings of the wedding processionals, ceremonies, and recessionals by Kyra Conley

All Scripture quotations, unless indicated, are taken from THE HOLY BIBLE: NEW INTER-NATIONAL VERSION®. Copyright © 1973, 1978, 1984 by International Bible Society. Used by permission of Zondervan Publishing House. All rights reserved.
Occasional uses of the Revised Standard Version and The Living Bible are indicated by the abbreviations RSV and LB respectively.

Most of the funeral portion of this book was previously published in 1990 by Baker Book House as *The Minister's Funeral Handbook*.

The Macmillan Publishing Company has given permission to use the following poetry of W.B. Yeats: "An Irishman Foresees His Death" and "When You Are Old" from *The Poems of W.B. Yeats: A New Edition*, edited by Richard J. Finneran. "Richard Cory" is taken from *The Children of the Night* by Edwin Arlington Robinson, © 1897 by Charles Scribner's Sons, New York.

Virginia Vanderford has given permission to use the poetry of Pearl Pierson; the Esta Bles eulogy is used with permission of Jeanne Bles; the William Dyerly material is used with permission of Beverly Ann Dyerly; and Charlie Bradshaw has given permission to use the poem, "From the Heart."

The following couples have graciously given permission for the inclusion of their wedding services: Leo & Chee Yin Blume, Bart R., Jr. & Cindy Pasini, and Patrick & Judy Whisnant. Tom Weber gave permission for use of his vows.

Library of Congress Cataloging-in-Publication Data

Blair, Robert, 1936–
    The funeral and wedding handbook / Robert Blair.— 2nd ed.
        p.   cm.
    Originally published: Joplin, Mo. : College Press Pub. Co., c1998.
    Includes bibliographical references. (p.).
    ISBN 0-7880-1882-5
    1. Death—Social aspects—United States. 2. Funeral rites and ceremonies—United States—Planning. 3. Weddings—United States—Planning. I. Title.
HQ1073.5.U6 B58 2002
306.9—dc21   2001052992
                                                                                    CIP

ISBN 0-7880-1882-5   PRINTED IN U.S.A.

Dedication

To my wife
Norma
who has given beautiful, loving, and faithful encourage-
ment for more than four and a half decades.
And to our children and their spouses:
Stephen and Pat, Rob and Julie,
Stephanie and Sean, Janice and Lloyd;
the grandchildren
Lyndsi, Jordan, Leslie,
Katie and her husband Trey, and Christina;
and my siblings
Doris and Carol (both deceased)
Marge, Don, and Gary.

I thank God for blessing me with their love.

Acknowledgments

The experiences for the wedding section of this handbook began over forty years ago when I officiated at my first ceremony. I'm indebted to many couples. I thank those who in the early years patiently endured the nervous mistakes caused by my inexperience. Fortunately, most of them stayed married despite the shaky nature of their wedding rites.

The members of the **Church of Christ in Hollywood** lent loving, spiritual support for twenty-eight years. **Avalyn VanCamp,** who served as church secretary for many years, gave me invaluable assistance and encouragement.

I'm grateful to **Bob Grupp** and **Gregg Johnson** for their advice with the manuscript and to **Julie Blair** for typing it. **Suzanne Willis** was an efficient proofreader.

I'm honored that **Wesley Runk, President of CSS Publishing Company** had faith in the book. And I appreciate **Tim Runk, Tom Lentz, Teresa Rhoads,** and others at **CSS** for their capable assistance and cooperation.

I shall always be grateful to my professors at **Central Christian College** (now **Oklahoma Christian University**) and **Pepperdine** for their unflagging faith in **Jesus,** and their respect for his eternal word.

God is so good.

The Funeral

HANDBOOK

Introduction

Why should you read a book on how to prepare a funeral sermon? No one gets off this planet alive. Death is inevitable. And, if you are a minister, preparing funeral eulogies is an inevitable part of your ministry.

You will be called on repeatedly to help people confront death and adjust to their grief, to speak words of comfort, and to enable them to go on living positive lives. What you say and how you say it can make a dramatic difference in the recovery of the survivors. The confidence you demonstrate and the message you bring will not only help the mourners, they can also lead to your own spiritual well-being and renewal. I say this because death not only takes families by surprise, it also takes the clergy by surprise. Suppose a tire on your car blows out on a strange road at night. If you have a jack, a spare tire, a flashlight, and a little mechanical knowledge, you probably suffer only a mild inconvenience. If you lack these basic tools, you are in for some heavy-duty frustration. This book does not have every answer to every question, but what I have tried to do is inform you of situations you will face and provide you with the basic tools I have developed over the past forty years.

This book is not only for ministers. The information should help anyone who is called to assist another in a time of grief. Often friends are guilty of giving the wrong advice about grief. They are usually present long before the minister or clergyperson. But what friends or ministers say and how they say it in those first few minutes can be crucial in the grieving process.

What qualifies me to write a book about funeral services and their preparation? It is more than just the experience of having done several hundred services over the past forty years. Not everyone who is thrown into the water becomes an adept swimmer. In my case I was thrown in so many times and the experience was so painful that for sheer sake of survival it was necessary that I develop some skills.

Is it expertise? Only partially. Each funeral is different, having unique parameters of emotion, family interaction, expressions of guilt and grief. I'm always learning.

A few years ago I scheduled a memorial service for an old friend at our church building on Sunday afternoon. I asked a younger associate if he planned to attend so that he could gain some experience. He said that he had planned not to be present. His response indicated that he did not want to be at the building while a dead body was there. One day he got his first request, as we all have, and he "enjoyed" that moment of sheer terror that many of us have experienced. Neither did I have any ambitions to be involved with funerals when I was young.

My first year of college was nearly an academic disaster. The following summer there were two significant changes in my life. First, following a stormy courtship, Norma finally agreed to marry me. Second, I decided to "become a minister."

The preacher who married us recommended that I attend a small Bible-based college in Oklahoma. It wasn't until my second semester there that I gained confidence in my academic abilities. However, at the time another event was shaping our lives: the birth of a son during the final exams in May.

Our funds were depleted. We rode the train home to Oregon. I had all the brashness and wisdom gleaned by any first-year Greek student. The little church where I grew up in

Oregon did not have a preacher for a time, so I was employed by them to preach each Sunday.

That was my preparation, my training for the first funeral service I preached. I had attended only one funeral in my life, that of a distant cousin who had committed suicide in Europe about the close of World War II. I recall some of the emotion of that service in the church building in a little Kansas town, but at age nine I was far more curious about other things. I was not much affected by such a remote thing as death. Because of the length of time between the death and the funeral we all were "spared" seeing the open coffin.

I do have vivid recollections of tracts published by my well-intentioned brethren in the Churches of Christ illustrating the teaching that proper baptism is burial in water. The only scriptural burial, they claimed, was dirt piled over one.

Did I hear sermons preached about funerals? I undoubtedly did. Did I see movies about funerals? Possibly, but I have no strong recollection or impression of them. I also suffered childhood nightmares of snakes and hellfire signifying death. Obviously, though, I was ill prepared for helping others to confront death.

To many of our blue-collar friends in that Portland suburb, I was ostensibly a death expert. After all, I had been to Bible college. The irony is, even in working toward my B.A. and M.A. in Religion, I still had no training in conducting funerals, and I don't know if it is part of the curriculum of any college in our brotherhood. But my friends in the community did not know that, and within a short period of time they were calling on me to fulfill my "pastoral duty."

The first call was most tragic. A former high school friend, one year younger than I, had been killed in an auto accident. I was the only minister the family knew. His elder brother had perfect confidence in me. Today, forty years later, I don't recall anything I said or might have said, or even where I got my resources. I believe I did call a couple of older minister friends to get their ideas on what to do and say. At some time I had picked up a minister's manual. However, my memory is not hazy on certain points. Vivid as though doubly etched yesterday is the recollection of my fear. It was a troubling, nauseating, morbid fear of death. I had not yet seen a corpse, and I was to be regarded as a "death expert."

I arrived at the funeral home early and was pacing back and forth through the lobby. The mortician was busy rearranging the chapel for the funeral in which I was to preach and wanted me out of the way. He escorted me to a little room off the lobby, suggesting that I meditate for a while. Without observing where I was, I sat down and began looking at my notes. I didn't look long. Right there in front of me, barely two feet away, was a corpse in a casket. It happened to be the remains of a woman in her mid-sixties, though I didn't stay long enough to gather details. I was out in the lobby again pacing the floor.

Did I offer any consolation to the family? I don't know. Did they receive any reassurance from the Word? I don't know that, either. But within a few days I got my second experience. An old family friend, a man in his late fifties, died of a heart attack one morning at work. I have no recollection of the service. I know one thing for sure. My fear of death was still unreasonably high.

At the end of another year my wife and I had saved sufficient funds so that we could move to Los Angeles where I finished school at Pepperdine College. As we were preparing to leave the Portland area, another old family friend, a woman in her early forties, was fighting a losing battle with cancer. I prayed long, fervent prayers the week before we left, not that God would heal her, but that the Lord would not let her die until we had moved. I did not want to deal with the reality of her death. The Lord did not grant my prayer.

After that, I was insulated from the problem for a while because of school and a brief tenure with an oil company. In 1963 I entered full-time ministry, but because I worked with an older, experienced minister, funerals were usually his responsibility. In 1966 he died. Almost overnight I had to prepare a memorial service for him.

In the period since, I've eulogized hundreds of persons. I was on call for several years to two of the largest mortuaries in

Southern California to do services for them in special circumstances.

Because Los Angeles is such a diverse community, I was invited to do services for people of numerous ethnic and cultural backgrounds. I eulogized some of my Jewish friends. There were services for stillborn babies and infants, and services for older millionaires.

In the funerals I have conducted in recent years I have set out to accomplish certain things. There are definite reasons for the funeral service beyond the need of the mortician to make a living. These have to do with using the sermon to proclaim the word about life in Jesus, to console the family by helping them remember the deceased, and to help them come to terms with death. All must be done in a proper order to be effective. In this small book I've offered suggestions on the minister's preparation of himself as well as the preparation of the service. I've also included some sample eulogies.

The only way to learn fully is by doing. However, funerals require delicate, tactful, and deliberate performance and delivery. They provide one of the few times when people are forced to consider soberly the brevity of life and their need to face God. What a unique opportunity to proclaim God's love. Be as prepared as possible before your first call.

POSTSCRIPT

Not long after this manuscript was accepted for publication, I encountered a funeral situation that easily held my swelling pride in check.

Without my knowledge a family scheduled a service at our church building. I became aware through various sources that several soloists and even a choir had been asked to participate. At the last minute I was asked to conduct the service.

It seemed as if the Lord was providing a test for me. After managing most of the complications associated with the service and even a few surprises, I felt almost proud of myself as the family slowly greeted one another outside the building and prepared to get into their cars for the seven-mile trip to the cemetery.

I felt confident and in charge as I entered the office to review a few last-minute things with the church secretary before the procession began.

The high ended for me abruptly. I walked out the door of the church building just in time to see the last car of the procession and the motorcycle escort drive away. I took several side streets, sweating profusely. The Lord rescued me again. I beat the procession by about three minutes.

Chapter One

PREPARING YOURSELF

There is a time to be born and a time to die.

If you plan to preach or to be in the ministry, you can expect to be asked to officiate at funerals. Also, you can expect that many of those funerals will come at the most inopportune times. Especially during my younger years, people seemed inclined to die a day or two before I was scheduled to go on vacation with my family. To tell a grieving family to whom you are close that you will be unavailable for a service for their loved one is not easy.

There is another unique factor about funerals. If you set a speaking engagement, you generally allow time for preparation. But it is a rare funeral that you know about many days in advance. In the case of Jewish services, burial is almost immediate. However, in the Los Angeles area where I lived, it is not uncommon for mortuaries to delay the services five days or more following the death. Given your other duties and necessary preparation, even five days may not seem long enough. If you have a morbid fear of corpses or death, you have your own emotional preparation to add.

How do you as a minister prepare yourself for that inevitable moment? It depends somewhat on how comfortable you feel in the presence of death. If your experience is no better than my first one, and you have never seen a corpse, this is the week, while you are reading this book, to see one. The sooner you face it the better. It's like the old saying: "If you have to swallow a frog, don't look at it too long."

If you want to be of consolation to grieving families, your own debilitating fears should be dealt with quickly. The best way to deal with them, I believe, is to call a local mortician, explain who you are, and ask him if he will help you by giving you a tour of his establishment. Chances are he'll be happy for the opportunity. He can show you what processes the body undergoes to prepare it for the service, such as embalming, cosmetology, and apparel. He can also show you how bodies are picked up from hospitals or other locations of death and explain what paperwork or arrangements may be necessary prior to his coming. In some cases, families may have to give written consent before a body can be released by a hospital to a mortuary. Also, the mortician can explain the types of services that are typically done in your area. Regional customs differ substantially. Some of these differences will be discussed later.

A visit to the funeral home will help you overcome your fears. It can also enable you to reassure the families that you will counsel and serve later. They will have many questions and concerns. If you can explain things competently, they will have greater confidence in you.

You may also want to attend a few services conducted by your peers. You can observe the strengths and weaknesses of their presentations and note the formats they use.

The most effective preparation of all, however, is to read the Word. Acquaint yourself with the promises of the Lord in Scripture concerning death and resurrection. Examine the way Jesus confronted death. He prepared his disciples for the inevitability of his own death by prophesying it (see Matthew 16:21, 20:18, and others). Note, too, the emotion with which he prayed in the garden. Death stands against life. It is the "wages of sin." Even the Son of God faced it in anguish and apparent trepidation. I've always been wary of poets' easy platitudes.

Yet it is not a time for despair if one is in Christ. Jesus won victory over death by his resurrection. Among the richest resources of the Bible are passages assuring that victory.

Among these are: Isaiah 25:6-8; John 5, 11, 14; 1 Corinthians 15; Romans 8; 1 Thessalonians 4, 5; and Revelation 7, 21, 22.

Before calling on a family, spend time in prayer. Tell God your fears. Ask for his wisdom and seek his consolation for the family.

It is possible that you have had long experience helping people through grief and you feel confident to help others face it. As I've gained experience, one hazard I've fallen victim to is being too sure of myself. My own overconfidence has led me at times to be insensitive to the pain of mourners. It is possible to be so clinical, professional, and experienced, that we are not humans. Remember, at the grave of Lazarus, "Jesus wept."

Chapter Two

PREPARING FOR
THE SERVICE

In Southern California, the greater number of funerals among the unchurched and Protestants is held in mortuary chapels. This is in contrast with many other parts of the country where most services are held in church buildings. I know of no spiritual reason why they should be held in church sanctuaries, but I can think of many practical reasons for conducting them in mortuary chapels, especially in urban areas. It can be hazardous to drive in long processions through the streets of large cities from the service to the burial place. The mortuary facilities are usually better suited for funeral arrangements than are church buildings. However, it is good to accommodate any family that prefers to use the church building.

Mortuaries in the Southern California area offer a full range of services besides providing chapels. They arrange to have ministers, all kinds of musicians, and could presumably have a stand-up comic if the family desired.

Many urban and rural churches have musical groups that specialize in providing music for funerals of members. I generally try to follow the wishes of the family in respect to music. I couldn't say how many times I've heard "The Old Rugged Cross," but if it consoles the family, it's okay with me.

I generally follow this format, which allows for variations:

Song (Optional)

Obituary

Reading of Scripture

Prayer

Song

Eulogy

Song

Prayer (If there is a graveside committal service, some families prefer not to have a closing prayer at the chapel or
church, but prayer is always appropriate.)

Even though the family gives obituary information to the
funeral director or counselor, I try to obtain it from the family
myself for several reasons. One of the most important is to
learn how to pronounce names of survivors (correct pronunci-
ation is crucial). Actually I regard every part of the service as
critical, because emotions are so tense. Second, funeral home
staffs frequently make typographical errors. Don't depend on
their correctness. A third reason to ask the family is that it
helps you to learn more about the deceased's situation.

Even though I might have been with the family at the time
of the death of their loved one, I try to make a separate
appointment to talk about the service. It's good to let them
know in advance why you are coming so they can gather any
information that might be helpful in preparing the eulogy.

When you meet with the family, get them to talk. Write
down everything you hear, even things that may not seem too
significant. Encourage them to reflect on their lives.

The session you have with the family serves another
important purpose. It helps you to understand their state of
mind and the particular needs you may have to address either
in the service or later.

What sort of information do you need and how do you
obtain it? To personalize the eulogy, you will need to familiarize yourself with the personality of the deceased through the
survivors' eyes. This can be difficult. In the first place, you
may barely know the family, and second, the circumstances

are far from normal. You may have to approach it from several different directions before you obtain what you need. It can require dogged persistence.

If you don't succeed in every case, don't feel that you have failed. There can be several reasons for failure, many of them not yours. I once spent more than an hour with a family for whom I had been asked to do a service. The father/husband had died. I met with the widow and two sons to get information for the service. As I tried to extract information, the conversation went something like this:

"Can you tell me something about your late husband's interests or hobbies?"

"He didn't have any. He just watched TV."

"Any special programs he liked?"

"No, he just watched everything."

"Can you tell me something about him that you remember best?"

"Nope. He was just an ordinary person."

Those people got an ordinary funeral. There was not much I could do about it.

I find it best to attempt to get the family comfortable with me first. It has been effective for me to briefly share some loss that I have experienced.

However, I believe it best not to say, "I know how you feel." Rather, you can share the pain and fear that you have experienced in similar circumstances. If you have never lost someone close to you, this is a little more difficult. But it is perfectly appropriate to say something like, "I know that what you are feeling right now must be very painful. Would it help to talk about it?"

The griever might say no. In that case you can suggest that you would like to talk later when the griever feels better. Tactfully explain that it will help you to conduct a more meaningful service if the family members can tell you a little about the one they have lost.

Most people are willing to talk. Often there are relatives present who are helpful. They are usually comfortable speaking to the griever, and you can take notes of their conversations.

There is a long list of sayings that well-intentioned people launch onto grieving people. When one of my sisters died about thirty years ago, I must have heard every trite saying there is, such as "God knows what is best." Not one of them helped. In some cases they got under my skin.

When Job's friends went to console him, they did the right thing for the first seven days. They didn't say a word. But once they started talking, they were of no more help than his nagging wife. A warm handshake, or a hug if you are familiar with the person, will express your love and concern better than any words. It is always appropriate to say that you will pray for the family. If they are believers (church members) you will not hesitate to say a prayer with them. If they are not members and you don't know their status, I think it wise to ask if they would like to have you pray with them.

One way to get the family to talk about the deceased is to be alert to photos and evidence of hobbies and interests in the home and to ask about them. You can ask about specific incidents or outings such as fishing trips or travel. You may focus on church work or activity in volunteer organizations, or the deceased's relationship with his/her children or grandchildren.

I once met with a family that had lost a mother/grandmother. As they began to reminisce, they laughed about her Brooklyn accent and the way she pronounced certain words. They also spoke of her appetite for pizza that she developed later in life. I made reference to both in the service. A little humor adds realism and also breaks the heavy tension that pervades so many funerals. Every human being has foibles. If the family makes reference to them, I usually take the liberty to make some comment. I do not refer to major difficulties such as problems with alcohol or mental illness, but if the person tended to be short tempered, it's a little ridiculous to say how much he or she loved everyone.

Several years ago a neighbor friend of ours died. He had owned and operated a small business in our community. At the service, the rabbi, who incidentally didn't know him, spoke about how the deceased had loved and respected everyone who came into his shop. When I had coffee with the store owner's son about a week after the funeral to see how he was adjusting, we spoke about the service. He noted that there were a few times he wanted to go check the coffin to make sure it was his dad the rabbi was talking about. His father definitely did not like everyone who came into his shop. In fact, he had tossed several people out. The son felt that the inaccurate comments had made the service seem unreal.

Be sure to take a note pad or a good supply of 4″ × 6″ cards. As you listen to the family reminisce and give you information, write down everything that is said. I prefer to use 4″ × 6″ cards or smaller pieces of paper so that in the office when I prepare the eulogy I can see all the information before me. This is better than having to turn sheets of paper back and forth. One other timesaving idea I've learned: I check off in my rough notes or strike through information as I use it so I'm not repeating material already used. Most family members commenting on the deceased will say, "She was a wonderful mother" or "I couldn't have asked for a better father." I try to be as faithful as my conscience will allow to the information given me. However, I believe it's wise to avoid overuse of superlatives. Too many "bests" and "greatests" can cause your comments to lose credibility.

Why do I so carefully gather this information? I believe it is important to personalize funerals as much as possible. One of the benefits is that it helps to induce weeping, thereby nurturing the grieving process. I attempt to do this by drawing a picture of the deceased as he or she was in life so that certain events and memories can be relived by the mourners. In another chapter I have included some sample services so you can see how I do it. It is not the only way, and I cannot claim that it is the best way, but it has been helpful to me.

I have established some principles for myself. First, I don't attempt to relegate anyone to hell or install anyone in the heavenly realms. As Paul said, "The sins of some men are conspicuous, pointing to judgment, but the sins of others appear later" (1 Timothy 5:24, RSV).

Once I went to the home of a man who had been active in our church to talk to his widow about funeral arrangements.

She warned me about saying good things about him. He was one of those who for years had fooled everyone but his wife and a few neighbors. As far as I know, no one in the church ever suspected he had a severe problem with gambling and other assorted vices. I surely had not.

It is always helpful to speak of specific things the deceased has done, just as the widows who showed "tunics and other garments which Dorcas made while she was with them" (Acts 9:39, RSV). But to assign a heavenly berth or cubicle of hell is not our place. I can't say for sure that anyone will be in heaven; only the Lord truly knows who are his. However, I can relate the person's witness of his or her faith.

In every instance, I try to accomplish the following without fail:

1. Funerals and memorial services are worship services. In every life situation we must acknowledge the rule of God. It's wise to remember this truth when we design funeral services. Survivors find it difficult to worship while they are grieving intently, but doing this will ultimately offer them the only real consolation. The hymns, prayers, Scriptures, and eulogies should accord with the theme of God's rule.

2. Utilize the natural tension and passion found in funeral settings. We should develop and utilize tension and passion in every talk or presentation that we make. What do I mean by the word **tension**? All good movies, stage productions, books, and speeches have tension in them. Tension refers to the conflict set up in the plot that remains unresolved until the last.

Thriller movies and novels keep us on the edge of our seats until the conclusion by either holding us in suspense about the identities of the perpetrators of the foul deeds, or by having the innocent characters in jeopardy until the last minute. Once we learn the identities of the bad guys or feel certain that the good people are safe, we put the novel down or leave the movie.

Soap operas utilize the principles of tension masterfully. Writers develop plots using nefarious characters, illnesses, and mishaps to keep lovers apart. Sometimes the stories unwind so slowly those soap fans tune in for years in the often-vain hope that their favorite leading characters will find happiness together.

Did Jesus use tension in his presentations? I think he did. The beatitudes epitomize it. Consider the conflict in the statement, "Happy (blessed) are those who mourn." Happiness and mourning seem totally opposite. As John 11 tells us, Jesus allowed the family of Lazarus to grieve for four days, and he wept with them, before he raised the dead man. Jesus also created unresolved tension by not explaining many of the parables. Each sermon that we preach or class that we teach must have this tension in order for us to retain the attention of our listeners.

Funerals have a natural tension that many ministers destroy at the outset. Doing this not only violates principles of speech; it's also not sound psychologically. I'm referring to the tendency of many ministers to begin funerals by saying, "We have come to celebrate the life of . . . ." Others authoritatively state, "Sister Susie is in heaven right now looking down on us." I'm not demeaning our hope of resurrection in Christ. But I think it's better to speak of that only after we help the mourners confront death and deal with their guilt.

It's good to maintain the tension respecting the awfulness of death until the close when we can offer the biblical hope of resurrection. Also, we help the mourners to understand that hope is available only when we come to terms with Jesus and who he is. After we remind them about what Jesus did for us, then we close with victorious, positive statements. It helps, too, if we quicken the pace of our delivery as we finish.

We should also present our lessons with passion indicating that we care. Often ministers drone with less feeling than a voice-mail message. At funerals and memorial services, people are often present who rarely, if ever, attend church. We have the unique privilege of presenting the most exciting news there is to them. But we do this expressively without sounding preachy, and we do it as briefly as possible. See point 5 and the Sample Eulogies for suggestions on how to present the good news of Jesus in funeral messages.

3. Help mourners come to terms with death. This is done by the use of Scripture that reminds us of the brevity of life. Poetry and quotations of people who have learned to recognize this are helpful — the more contemporary the source, the better. Mourners must be brought to the "brink of the grave" and encouraged to face the horrible reality of death, not to practice denial.

4. Induce mourning. Draw verbal pictures of the life and activities of the deceased. On numerous occasions, I have asked friends of the deceased to help do this by speaking for three to five minutes. I tell them specifically what I would like them to do and how much time they should take. I've never had anyone abuse the opportunity.

5. Deal with guilt. Guilt will be felt to some extent by all the mourners. Urge them to confess it to God — according to 1 John 1:9. Tell them of the guilt you have felt in various circumstances and how good it feels to be forgiven in Christ.

6. Encourage active participation by the mourners. If the mourners listen to a solo or organist and hear readings, prayers, and a eulogy by you, their experience will be entirely passive. Their active participation will enhance their ability to deal with their grief. How can you actively involve the mourners? Use responsive readings or have them recite a familiar psalm with you. Encourage congregational singing. In the case of small gatherings, you can encourage each of the mourners to relate some experiences (see chapter on alternative services).

7. Present living hope in Christ. I generally introduce this by saying something like the following:

"How can we prepare ourselves for times like today? We need to have our own lives in readiness.

"How is this done? We must come to terms with who Jesus is. He was not just another man, not just a good teacher or philosopher. He was sent from God and is uniquely God's Son.

"He lived a perfect life that accomplished at least two things. First, by his example he demonstrated the content of a perfect life of love, humility, courage, purity, and faithfulness to God. Second, he successfully resisted all temptation. He was tempted in every way, just as we are — yet he was without sin (see Hebrews 4:15).

"When Jesus was executed it was for our failures, not his. He paid the penalty we deserve."

I then briefly explain the heart of the good news about Jesus, using the basic points in the sermons found in the Book of Acts: (1) God sent Jesus into the world; (2) we crucified him; (3) God raised him on the third day; (4) He ascended to the right hand of God; (5) salvation is only in him; (6) he will return to judge the world by his righteousness.

I also explain how we can share in his resurrection if we are in him. I rely heavily on the following passages: 1 Corinthians 15, 2 Corinthians 5, 1 Thessalonians 4:13-18. I recall how impressed a nonbelieving doctor was at the reading from 1 Corinthians 15 during a service for his wife, who was a believer. His rational mind was deeply convicted by the proofs of Jesus' resurrection that Paul delineates in the first several verses. As I read Paul's reminder that more than five hundred witnesses, most of whom were still alive at his writing, had seen Jesus at once, I could hear the old doctor say to his son, "I like that."

The message about Jesus is convicting. It is life.

Chapter Three

WHEN YOU ARE THE
BEARER OF BAD NEWS

On some occasions it will be your unenviable responsibility to inform the family of the death of one of their members. Few occasions require more prayerful tact, wisdom, and sensitivity.

Not long ago, I had to call the daughter of an old friend to tell her that I had found her father dead on the floor of his apartment. The daughter lived out of state. When I called her, my first words were: "I've got some bad news for you." She could tell from the tone of my voice what the bad news was and queried me further about the details. In her case, I knew her family well and was confident of her ability to handle the information by herself. If the family were within driving distance, I would not phone but simply go directly to the home of the survivors to tell them in person.

WHEN YOU TELL THEM

Should they be standing or sitting when you tell them? It's best to have them sit and then give them the information in as tender, straightforward terms as you can. Some people will possibly faint or collapse at the news. If they are sitting, there is far less likelihood of injury.

Many, however, will get up immediately and start to pace nervously. If you have experienced the death of a loved one, you know the numbing sensation that sets in immediately. The news is too horrible to accept in one course, and your mind and body begin the long process of acceptance that has been so well described by Elisabeth Kübler-Ross and others. Because of fear and shock there will be great surges of adrenalin. Some motor functions may be impaired.

It is my opinion that mourners should be encouraged to weep as much as possible. Walk with them to help them work off some of the pent-up energy. It is far healthier to weep openly and expressively than to maintain a public stoicism. Those who weep will get past the grief process far more effectively and completely.

Though I run the risk of being at odds with some in the medical profession, neither do I believe that tranquilizers are healthy. The Lord made the process of grief that has been effective for thousands of years. The use of tranquilizers only suppresses or retards the natural process.

Let's say that sister A and sister B lose a brother. Sister A reacts by screaming and crying out "No! No!" for several minutes, then continues to sob almost convulsively for hours.

Sister B, on the other hand, accepts the news quietly and sits misty eyed for a time, but soon joins with others in consoling sister A. Which sister is doing better? If you asked most people, they would say sister B is handling the situation well. Generalizations can be dangerous, because no two people ever react the same way to any news, good or bad. But if sister B is quiet because she is suppressing her grief, the more vocal sister A will probably adjust faster and more completely.

Women can often handle grief much more effectively than men, because there are fewer social or cultural restrictions against public demonstrations of weeping by women. Both in counseling families on the day of the death of a loved one and at funerals, too, I encourage weeping as much as possible.

How do you encourage people to cry?

First, you give permission by telling them it's all right, perfectly natural to weep. Second, you induce weeping by talking as much as possible about their lost loved one.

If you knew the deceased, you can speak of your recollections and attempt to converse with the family to encourage their reflection. If you did not know the deceased, you can simply say, "Tell me something about your sister. What do you remember best about her?"

If you knew the deceased, it is helpful to relate experiences that you shared. In Acts 9:36, Tabitha (Dorcas) has just died. She had been an extraordinary woman, "who was always doing good and helping the poor." Her loved ones had washed her body and were weeping over it. When Peter arrived "he was taken upstairs to the room. All the widows stood around him, crying and showing him the robes and other clothing that Dorcas had made while she was still with them."

What the widows did enabled the grief process. The clothing they displayed helped them to remember Dorcas and her good deeds. Possibly one said, "Dorcas made this gown for me last month when I was sick." Another would say, "Just after my husband died, Dorcas brought me this beautiful tunic she had made."

It helps to recollect the good deeds of the deceased. "He used to drive me to the doctor," or "She volunteered several hours a week to feed the hungry people on Main Street. I recall what joy it brought her to serve."

However, don't talk too much and don't talk too soon. When loved ones are first told, they may just need a good shoulder to cry on for a while. Let them cry as long as they like. If the grieving person is young, and you are young (or even old) and of the opposite sex, it's a good idea to have someone else with you. If it is a woman you are visiting, and you are a man, take two or more of the sisters from the church to be in the home with you. Emotions are extremely complex. Fires of passion can be aroused in times of grief. This is not the time to get life more complicated for you or the griever.

Don't try to minimize the importance of the loved one's loss and don't offer clichés about it being God's will. In fact, it is best to keep advice to an absolute minimum. Simply be a quiet, concerned friend.

What is appropriate to say? Brief readings of Scripture are always the best counsel. Psalms 23 or 91 and 1 Corinthians 15 are very helpful. You can pray with the bereaved, helping them to verbalize the pain they feel. It is good for them to honestly express their pain.

David was famous for telling God of his anger and disappointment. Psalm 60 begins with his typical honest frustration: "You have rejected us, O God, and burst forth upon us; you have been angry — now restore us!"

One way to assist grievers toward honest expression is by your own candor. Tell of your pain in a similar circumstance. You may want to take mental notes, if not paper-and-pencil notes, of what is said so it can be dealt with at more length later and to make sure that all the bitterness eventually gets worked through.

How do you determine when it is appropriate for you to leave? You will have to use your judgment based on the answers to some simple questions. Does the griever agree with the idea when you say you are about to leave? Are there family members, church members, or close friends present who can assist when you depart? Has the griever worked through the initial highly emotional reaction? Those who stay should be advised that the best therapy is S.A.S. (sit and be silent) so the griever will have time to reflect and sob.

THINKING ABOUT DETAILS

Usually the family needs help in several ways. Relatives should be notified. The grief sitter can ask, "Would you like some help in calling your loved ones?" The griever can help list the names and tell where the numbers can be found.

Funeral arrangements should be made. Has the deceased made prior arrangements? If so, where are the instructions? Has a mortuary been selected? It would be wise for you as a minister to know of a couple of reputable firms to which grievers can be referred. If you give them the names of two or more, you will be above possible accusations of collusion with the mortuary. It is good for someone to go to the mortuary with the griever.

In the case of large families, accommodating visiting mourners can be a real but necessary chore. A concerned and organized friend should be identified who can coordinate arrangements for out-of-town relatives, meet them at the airport, and find lodging for them while they are in town.

The family will need help immediately in other ways, too. The process of grieving requires great energy. The mind is so busy grappling with the ugliness of death, attempting to accept it, and coming to terms with it, that there can be little physical energy left. Grievers are often disorganized, disoriented, and unable to plan the smallest of tasks. Church members can render a good ministry in the grief process by assisting with dishes, cooking meals, cleaning house, answering the door, and calling relatives. Obviously, the privacy of the mourners must be respected. However, the above are areas where mourners are often happy to receive help. There will be some who will prefer to handle all matters by themselves. Tactfully respect their needs.

In rural communities, traditions have often been established so that help has been given to the mourners in the same way for generations. Urban communities often lack these traditions, but the church or other organizations can fill a needed role. You can do yourself and your church an important service by setting some systems in place to be ready when they are needed.

If you are new in your community, talk with some of the old-timers to discover what the local traditions are. In some communities wakes are still a standard practice.

To know what your resources are for transportation, food, assistance with housework, etc., encourage your deacons to conduct a survey of your church members. It will assist you to identify those who can be called in time of need.

I spoke with a Catholic woman in her early forties whose mother died suddenly. They had lived together for many years. The mother did not answer the phone when the daughter called from work to find out how she was doing. The daughter went to the house and found her mother dead on the floor. When she called her church, no priest was available. But the parish sent a woman, a volunteer experienced in dealing with situations like the one my friend was undergoing. This volunteer performed a good ministry. It helps to have a group of volunteers who can be mobilized quickly to deal with circumstances of grief.

DEALING WITH GUILT

One of the strongest emotions connected with death is guilt. It is almost universally expressed. Guilt is felt even where the relationships have been good and wholesome. It is the nature of human beings to leave things unsaid and undone. There are matters you intend to discuss with your spouse but haven't yet broached. You intend to do things with or for your spouse that you haven't done. If your spouse dies with these things unresolved, it poses a real dilemma. It leaves you unable to make amends. Husbands and wives leave the house in the morning having had harsh words with their spouses. Sometimes they don't return. When they don't, it leaves the survivor with a crushing load of guilt.

In 1966, there was a series of deaths of persons close to me. In the case of each one there was unresolved guilt. That guilt exacerbated other inadequacies I felt at the time. It took several months for me to work through it. It would have been much easier had someone explained to me that it is normal to feel that way.

It is necessary to explain how normal the presence of guilt is. It is also important to provide some means of coping with it realistically. Frequently counselors will tell grievers not to worry about guilt. That doesn't make the guilt go away. They need to feel forgiven by the Lord. First John 1:9, "If we confess our sins, he is faithful and just and will forgive us our sins and purify us from all unrighteousness," has been of great consolation to me. Help mourners to verbalize their feelings to the Lord and to ask for forgiveness.

DEALING WITH CHILDREN

What do you say to children? It's best, I think, to keep children informed. Tell them honestly. Answer their questions in a simple, straightforward manner. I don't think we should try to hide things from them. They sense things. They also have vivid imaginations.

Some years ago I met a family at a funeral home. The grandmother had died, and the family had gathered to view her remains in the "slumber room." The deceased's daughter was the mother of a girl about five years old. The family was preparing to go to the slumber room, and the little girl wanted to go along. The mother didn't want her to go. She believed that little children should not be exposed to death. I encouraged her to take the child with her. What the child imagined about death — what was in that mysterious room about which everyone spoke in whispers — would have been far worse than anything the child actually saw. There was no evidence that she suffered any from the experience. It was quite the contrary.

When our children were small, they attended funerals with us. Children are far more apt to verbalize their fears than adults. When they do, you can address them. Our four children were between the ages of four and ten when one of their cousins died of sudden infant death syndrome at eighteen months. It was a difficult night for our youngsters. They remembered having seen the little boy the summer before on our vacation. Our ten-year-old son was the most upset.

As I began talking with him, I recognized that his greatest fear was for his cousin's fate. When I explained to him that no little child who dies will ever leave God's care, that God loves them, and that they will be in heaven with him, he stopped his sobbing and in just a short time fell asleep.

To be honest, if I did not believe that, I don't know what I would or could say to children or adults.

LEAVING GRIEVERS ALONE

Should the griever be left to himself or herself? In most cases space and time should be provided for grievers to be alone. They need time to work through their loss. Advise them to reflect quietly on the deceased, to try to remember good times and bad times. They may repeatedly relive certain incidents. It is not morbid. This is the natural process for coming to terms with the loss.

The following should never be left alone:

1. Minors. The first thing to do is to get legal counsel if minors within your church family have been orphaned. If you have had no experience in this area, be sure to consult a trustworthy person who has. Keep names on hand of people who are qualified in this area.

2. Suicidal persons. How do you know if a person is suicidal? If that person is reputed to be or has talked of it, you are well advised to consult a fully trained counselor. Be especially wary if the person has indicated to you what method of suicide he or she intends to use — knife, razor blades, gas etc. If someone has thought about it to the degree that he or she has considered a means, take the threat especially seriously.

3. Infirm or extremely elderly people. Several persons have consulted me recently on dealing with their mates who have Alzheimer's disease. Their concern is that if they should die first, who will help care for the surviving spouse who is afflicted with Alzheimer's. It is important to have written instructions beforehand and to proceed with legal counsel. Obtain clarification and accord of the family members. Files containing instructions can be placed for easy access in the church office.

ONE FINAL IMPORTANT POINT

Do not necessarily assume that you will be the officiant at the funeral. Sometimes the family has an old friend or a favorite uncle or aunt or a son-in-law who is a minister. They may have already made a commitment to have that person officiate.

The best way to clarify it is to state sincerely that you will be glad to help in any way you can. Usually at that point they will ask you to do the service. Then you can make an appointment with them to return and discuss the arrangements.

In the event they do not respond by clarifying their intentions, you can ask something like the following: "Have you made arrangements for a minister to officiate, or would you like for me to help you?"

Before you leave the home, pray with the mourners. Set an appointment for a time mutually convenient when you can return to discuss funeral arrangements.

Chapter Four

LEGAL QUESTIONS
AND MORTUARIES

Some of the nastiest and most perplexing problems surrounding death are the legal and financial questions that arise. Two of the most difficult legal questions have to do with autopsies and embalming. Because laws vary from state to state, you will have to investigate which laws apply locally. In California presently, if a person has not seen a physician for a prescribed length of time, an autopsy is required. Contrary to some popular myths, an autopsy does not require total dismemberment or disfigurement of the body. In fact, most of the time no layman could tell that an autopsy had been performed.

In certain cases, hospitals may want to perform autopsies for different reasons, some having to do with medical advancement and training. They usually obtain family permission.

Some years ago, a little boy about six years old, whose family attended our church, developed a virulent form of cancer. He was hospitalized in one of the facilities in Los Angeles that treats children. The family had limited income and probably was charged very little if any for the several weeks of medical inpatient treatment at the hospital. When the little boy died, the medical staff at the hospital put tremendous pressure on the mother to allow an autopsy on the child. Though I felt bad for the people at the hospital who would benefit from the training, their approach to the mother caused her so much stress that I helped her resist the pressure.

The family may get pressure from another source. In this case it is very subtle. For that reason it can be even more difficult to resist. A family may shift from being very angry with doctors or others they feel are connected with their loved one's death to feeling overwhelming guilt. One way to "make up" for wrongs to or neglect of the departed one is to have a "nice funeral." Guilt makes people susceptible to doing things they would not ordinarily do.

A casket cannot help a corpse. A corpse can't feel, sense, see, smell, or hear anything. It will, in a fairly short time, be dust. But logic rarely prevails in the purchase of a casket unless unemotional heads have prevailed prior to death. Most mortuaries are operated, I believe, by basically honest people. It is true that most morticians do not stand over you insisting that you purchase their deluxe models of copper caskets supplied with inner spring mattresses, satin, lace, and double sealed liners to keep out the elements. It's also true that they don't twist your arm to sell you the lot that is under the shady oak tree or at the top of the hill overlooking the whole valley. But what they tend to do is to show you the expensive models and lots first. After you have seen the deluxe ones, you are shown the cheap ones. They are drab in contrast. Remember that guilt? "Nothing is too good for our mother!"

Imagine going to an auto showroom where in the most prominent, visible location are expensive Rolls-Royces, Mercedes, and other luxury cars. After you have admired these, you are shown several rows of sports cars, then mid-sized cars. Far in the back, almost in the dark area, are a few economy models. Suppose you had promised your mother you would buy her a car, and she went to the showroom with you. Even if you could afford nothing but the cheapest economy model, you would probably still feel cheap after you had seen the Rolls-Royce and Mercedes-Benz models. That's part of the pressure you are under in the casket selection room.

A friend of ours of modest income who attends another church lost her mother. She called asking my advice on the selection of a funeral home. I gave her the names of a couple of mortuaries and also forewarned her about the sales techniques that she could expect. She thanked me for the advice. She was afraid, she said, that she would be taken advantage of and she wanted my assistance in resisting the pressures. I was satisfied that she understood the warnings and precautions I advised.

At the funeral service I was amazed to see that she had selected one of the most expensive caskets available for her mother. Where did I fail? I still don't know.

In other cases I have been somewhat more successful but have paid a price. I mentioned earlier that I was on call for two of the largest mortuaries in Southern California to do services for persons who desired a Church of Christ minister but who were not members of a particular congregation. I also did services at these mortuaries for other persons who had no church background. The family simply requested a minister, and the mortuary arranged for me to come.

All of that came to an end several years ago when a member of our church, a grandmother in her seventies, died. The woman's daughter was in failing health. The granddaughters had to make arrangements for the funeral. They were in their early twenties, had little business experience, and no experience in arranging for funerals. They asked me to accompany them.

After all the information had been obtained by the counselor, it was time to go to the casket selection room. On entering the room, we were greeted by the presence of all those luxury models I have described. The daughters immediately fell in love with one. It cost several thousand dollars. I suggested that they might want to look a little further. They agreed. The counselor was exasperated by the potential loss of commission, but told the young women that he would step outside so they would be free to choose whatever casket they wished.

After he had gone, I asked the young women about their ability to pay for the casket. They were of limited income and would have had to finance a great share of the cost. I suggested to them that the casket would not help their grandmother. It would be buried, and their only reminder would be a long series of payments. They finally agreed on a moderately priced casket. It was considerably narrower than the one they had originally admired. The new casket was still more expensive than they could afford, but given their state of mind I doubted whether they could have accepted a cheaper looking casket.

When the counselor reappeared, he was visibly chagrined by their choice. Not yet having given up, he approached the casket they had chosen, remarking, "The choice is entirely yours, of course, but remember (at that moment he drew a tape measure out of his pocket and started measuring the inside width of the casket) your grandmother is a woman of considerable girth. I'm not sure she will fit in this casket." I drew him aside and insisted, "I'm sure you can squeeze her in." They did. The mortuary stopped calling me to do services after that.

If you know that the family has limited income and no previous arrangements have been made, you may want to accompany the surviving family members to help them to survive financially. But another precaution: you don't want to increase the family's stress by causing a conflict with the mortician.

The answer may well be to have some class sessions for church members on dealing with funeral arrangements and money management.

Is it necessary to embalm? At present in California it is not necessary if burial takes place within the state. However, for shipment out of state for burial, corpses must be embalmed. What is embalming? It consists mainly of draining blood and pumping a preservative solution through the veins.

The family will encounter many other choices. These include whether to purchase flowers to cover the casket, and how much should be spent for them; whether to have flowers present in the room where the corpse resides prior to the funeral; whether to have limousine service; whether a vault is necessary, and what type of interment there will be.

Because caskets eventually collapse, causing the lawn surface to sink, some cemeteries require a concrete liner or vault for the casket's exterior. These come in high- and low-priced models. Be aware that morticians speak of "protection" — protection for a body that will never feel a thing again and will eventually be dust.

What about cremation? Cremation was once the choice of a few persons noted for their idiosyncrasies. It is becoming increasingly popular. It is definitely not the emotional issue it once was. Cremation saves expenses of burial and real estate, and also in some cases saves expense of the casket. Some people I've talked with worry about the loss of the body for resurrection purposes. In my opinion it is no more difficult for the Lord to raise a body which has been consumed by fire than it is for him to raise a body which has been dead five days. All things are possible for him.

Chapter Five

TERMINAL ILLNESS AND PREDEATH SITUATIONS

One of the most telling factors in the way we handle grief is the manner in which we prepare for it. It is somewhat like preparing for retirement. Some people don't want to think about it until the day it takes place. They meet it totally unprepared.

There are many middle-aged people in our country whose parents have been confined for years in convalescent homes. Many of them will be no better prepared for their parents' deaths than a Midwesterner is for a tidal wave.

Two areas of concern will be treated in this chapter. First, should a dying person be told that he will die? Second, how does the family prepare when one of its members has a terminal illness?

The first question deals with a many-sided issue. Occasionally, medical societies and other special-interest groups hold seminars on the subject. It would be helpful to take advantage of these opportunities.

A number of years ago, I was trapped in a nasty dilemma while dealing with the stepfather of an old school friend. He had cancer, but for some reason the physician had never told him how serious it was. His wife asked me to visit him. I called on him almost weekly for several months in their home. His condition progressively worsened, but he always spoke of recovery.

One day the wife walked me to the door and begged me to help her. Her husband had never made out a will, which meant at that time in California that the estate would be tied up in probate unless he did something about it. His physician, however, had ordered that he not be informed that his condition was terminal. His doctor was probably one of the few persons unable to come to terms with death himself.

The wife was afraid to disobey the doctor's order, but at the same time seemed to be in jeopardy of substantial financial loss if her husband died without preparing a will. My naiveté and inexperience left me very insecure in that situation. After agonizing over the question for a long time, I finally sought help from my physician and an attorney friend.

We arrived at this solution. Instead of singling out just the dying husband, I was to speak to the two of them together, pointing out that in view of their age it was important that they have wills prepared to make sure that their wishes would be carried out. The husband did query me as to why I brought up the subject. I was able to respond in all sincerity that both of them needed to have their affairs in order because of their age.

As it turned out, he had prepared the property deed so that it was not a problem for the wife. However, she had no way of knowing that he had taken care of it prior to the conversation.

Is it wise to tell a person that his or her condition is terminal? There are strong arguments on both sides. I believe the dying should be told of the seriousness of their condition. They need to have frank, open discussions with their loved ones. The family members need also to resolve any conflicts they may have had with the patient.

On the other hand, who can state with certainty when death will come? Over thirty years ago, my niece was suffering from a rare childhood disease. Doctors had given her only a few months to live. She lived in the Pacific Northwest. One of my sisters, the girl's aunt, thought it would be a great idea to bring our niece to Los Angeles and take her to Disneyland so she could have one last wish before she died. I remember accompanying them. I fought back tears the whole day, convinced that I was seeing her alive for the last time.

There was a death within the next several months, but it was not my niece's. It was my sister's — the one who had arranged the Disneyland trip for our niece. And my niece, how is she doing? I had the honor of performing her wedding ceremony a few years ago in Portland. She and her husband now have two children of their own.

Another point to consider is that it is possible to destroy one's will to live by telling him with too much certainty what his prognosis is. In each instance it is a question to which doctors, family, and ministers should give much prayer and careful thought.

How do you prepare a family when the death of a loved one is reasonably certain or near? It is, I believe, necessary to first broach the subject by asking a question like, "Have you considered what life will be like when _____ is not here?" The reaction to that question will give you clues as to how to proceed. Tears may come to their eyes, or you might get a response such as, "I don't want to think about it!"

It would be helpful for you to relate your own fears. This will enable family members to open up to you so you can identify what their real anxieties are. In some cases you may fail to accomplish this. You may hint, suggest, or even talk bluntly to no avail. Some people absolutely refuse to think about death. If you have made a thoughtful, loving, prayerful attempt and don't succeed, don't blame yourself too harshly. It is not easy to undo years of conditioning.

I have left the most important thing until last. No person should ever be in our presence very long without hearing the comforting, consoling message of good news about Jesus. It's the greatest help of all in every circumstance.

In the case of my friend's father, I may have been successful in dealing with his wife's legal-financial problem, but I hardly dealt with the greater issue of death at all. To be sure, all of us have a responsibility to free our loved ones from legal complications by leaving our houses in order. But there is a larger and greater issue. Why didn't my friend's father know, or admit that he knew (if he did know), that he was dying? Some of us don't know too much; yet there is one thing that we should know: our own bodies.

If we have been told that we have cancer involving some vital organ, and if that organ should be so adversely affected that bodily functions are seriously impaired, it ought to be a sure clue that we may have a limited number of days. It seems to me that we should know our own bodies well enough to have some understanding or inkling of the seriousness of the problem we face. What I'm suggesting is that the evidence should have been overwhelming to my friend's father that he was dying. Yet for some reason he missed or avoided all the clues. Was it because he sensed everyone else was avoiding it, too, so that he couldn't bring himself to the point of openly discussing a subject that frightened everyone else? It is quite possible that the condition was created just as much by the dread expressed, albeit nonverbally, by the family, the doctor, and me as by the dying man's fear.

Actually, many dying persons are able to come to terms with their conditions and carry on frank, open discussions with those close to them. Some of the most candid, intriguing discussions I've ever had were with two different friends — one who was dying from leukemia and the other from Lou Gehrig's disease (amyotrophic lateral sclerosis).

It will be of great help to the family later, as well as immediately helpful to the terminally ill person, if candid conversations can be encouraged. Members of the family can speak about their love and appreciation for their loved ones. They may eventually become comfortable enough to clear up any misunderstandings that may have existed. And it lets the dying person know he or she is not dying alone. A minister is in a unique position to guide a family in this.

Chapter Six

GRAVESIDE SERVICES

It is customary to conclude a service at the place of interment. This may be at the graveside, mausoleum, or niche where ashes are placed.

Usually there is a cortege, that is, an auto procession. At some cemeteries in which funeral services are held in chapels on the grounds, you may simply walk to the place of interment.

At the close of the service it takes the mortuary personnel a few minutes to remove the flowers, transport them to the cemetery, and place them at the graveside. Funeral directors like to have the flowers placed before the family arrives. You can use the time to ready your notes and read over the Scriptures you plan to use at the committal service. If you are unfamiliar with the mortuary, ask the director out of which door they will take the casket. You don't want to be standing by yourself in front of the chapel while they are loading the hearse in the rear.

When the mortician has everything ready, he will wheel the casket toward the exit where the pallbearers are waiting. Or the pallbearers may carry or escort it from its resting place in the chapel. Customs on this vary from place to place. You should walk a few paces in front of the casket until you reach the funeral coach (hearse). Stand out of the way facing the casket until it is placed in the coach and then return to your car.

In some parts of the country it is customary for the mourners to follow the casket from the church building or mortuary. Check with mortuary personnel or an older minister in your area to determine local customs.

Most directors will arrange for the minister to have a prominent place in the cortege. I've noticed that many younger directors are less attentive to detail, so possibly no one will reserve a place for you. Should you insist on it? If you feel that it is important to you, do it. However, I think the Lord has called me to be a servant, so if I'm not given a prominent position, I go to the back of the procession. If you are disabled or if the time element is crucial, explain it to the director ahead of time.

When you arrive at the place of interment you can, as soon as you park the car, go quickly to the rear of the funeral coach and stand in attendance until the casket is removed by the pallbearers. Be sure to ask the director ahead of time to point out the correct grave site and which route the procession will take. You will feel a little stupid heading toward the wrong open grave. Also ask which direction the casket will face. As you lead the procession to the grave, it helps to look back occasionally to see if they are keeping pace or are about to bump into you.

When you arrive at the grave site, stand at the foot of the grave, giving ample room for the pallbearers to place the casket. I've also learned that it's a good idea to watch the pallbearers carefully. The footing is often precarious around a grave, and they are carrying a heavy load. Occasionally you may give assistance.

Usually the director will signal you when everything is in readiness and it is time to start. It generally takes a while for all the mourners to assemble. I have found it helpful to get myself ready then by praying quietly and reflecting on how I will begin.

It is often necessary to request people to gather in closer. Remember, you will not have the benefit of a public address system, and there will be various outside noises including wind, rain, and airplanes. Use your strongest voice. To be sure you will be heard, you can ask someone (not a member of the immediate family) to stand toward the back and signal to you whether your voice volume is adequate.

If there has already been a service at the mortuary or church building, I usually read a few Scripture passages, recite or read an appropriate poem, and then have a concluding prayer.

If there has been no service at the chapel, you will likely want to give a brief eulogy. (Sample prayers, readings, and eulogies are given in chapter 10.)

Graveside committal services most often end with prayer. When you have concluded, nod to the director, step to the foot of the casket if you are not already there, and the director will take over. Customs vary. Some people sprinkle soil on the casket and say, "Dust thou art. . . ." in other localities the casket is buried completely before the family leaves. In some areas it is customary for the pallbearers to place their boutonnieres on the casket. The director will take care of this ceremony. If the deceased was a veteran, an American flag is often draped over the casket. At the close of the service the director will fold the flag and hand it to a family member. As soon as these ceremonies are over, it is appropriate for you to walk over to where the family is sitting or standing and offer a firm handshake or a hug, depending on your familiarity with them. The mourners can then offer their condolences to the family.

How long should you stay at the graveside? This depends on how well you know the family, what their needs are, and your own schedule. If you are close to the family and they have few friends or no one else to give support, you may want to stay. If you have simply been "hired" by the mortuary to do the service, ask the immediate survivors if you can help them in any way. Usually they will say no.

In some cases family members or friends will have a meal or gathering at the home or church hall of the deceased or a family member. The type of gathering can range from very solemn to very wild and raucous depending on the culture or family. If they invite you, it is proper to go, but do not be the last to leave. You must be the monitor of your time. If I believe I can be of assistance to the mourners by my presence, or if I have an opportunity to declare my faith in Jesus, I will go. My decision obviously also depends on my schedule. Many times I have gone directly from a funeral to a wedding.

Before I leave I always ask the immediate survivors if I can be of further assistance. At times they will have questions. You can make a follow-up appointment in a few days. Keep your promise if you say you will call. You will experience a range of responses when you do call back. (These will be discussed in chapter 9.)

I believe one of the greatest services you can render is to be observant of other family members who have special needs. At times a child will be especially baffled and pained by what is going on. Children have many questions. Often adults don't see their needs because of their own grief. If you see someone standing quietly off to one side, you are likely seeing someone in great need. You may be the right one to minister to such persons.

Chapter Seven

ALTERNATIVE
SERVICES

Funerals are very expensive. They are also a custom which many people do not want to follow. Sometimes this decision is based on finances, sometimes not. What can you do in the event you are dealing with a family whose wishes differ from the norm?

I believe that some of the nontraditional forms of services can be among the most helpful. I dealt with a family who had lost a grandfather. He had not wanted a funeral. Yet there was a need for the family somehow to deal with their grief, and they asked for my help.

We arranged to have a family gathering. The wife and daughter, the son-in-law, the granddaughters, and their husbands all met with me in the daughter's home one evening. (The grandfather's body had already been cremated.) I read a few Scripture passages and then asked each of the family members to share their best recollections of the deceased. We were sitting in a circle in the living room, and each shared in turn some event or memorable time. They laughed and cried and laughed and cried some more. After they all had an opportunity to share, we closed with a prayer together. I think it was one of the most meaningful services I ever did, and I said so to that family.

A couple in their late thirties who attended our church several years ago looked forward to the birth of their first child.

The baby boy was stillborn and his infant body cremated. The parents wanted to have a small service for him, but could not afford a funeral. We drove to a spot on a hillside overlooking the city. After I said a few words of consolation and prayed with them, they scattered the ashes and flowers down the hillside. It was one of the saddest occasions of my life and, obviously, very different from any other funeral service.

In some areas there is a growing custom to have a private burial service at the cemetery with only the immediate family members present. Later (that evening or a day or two following the burial) a memorial (or victory celebration) service is held in the deceased's church building.

When deciding alternatives to traditional services, the questions I ask myself are first, is it biblical, and second, is it legal? What does the family really want? Does this violate my conscience or compromise my beliefs in any way? Will what I do help them to grieve and to come to greater faith in God?

Having answered these questions I don't worry a lot about convention and custom.

Chapter Eight

HELPFUL HINTS

FOR THE DAY OF THE FUNERAL

BE PREPARED

You will enhance your confidence on the day of the funeral if you have finished your preparation for the service the day before. I occasionally extemporize talks but never a eulogy. I write out all the details and words. Perhaps after some years you will feel more confident than I do, but feelings are too sensitive and the atmosphere too heavy with emotion for mistakes. Gravediggers may cover the body afterward, but you will have a difficult time "covering" mistakes due to lack of preparation. Besides preparing your own part, make sure soloists, organists, and others know at what time of the service they will be needed.

REVIEW

Review your notes of order of service and eulogy before you go to the service and once you arrive. Try to have the outline and what you are doing firmly in your mind.

BE EARLY

I try to be at the place of service at least twenty minutes in advance. At times the family has last-minute requests, or you may need to clarify certain items. Sometimes they will recall an incident about Aunt Jane when she was twelve years old that they want mentioned. Or they will recall that Uncle Charlie's favorite Scripture was Psalm 23. Early arrival will help you take care of these last-minute requests.

GET ACQUAINTED

If you have not yet seen the deceased, go into the chapel or church building and stand a few minutes by the casket. This will enable you to be past the initial shock when the service starts. In addition, if you are not acquainted with the chapel, it helps to know where you will stand and/or sit during the service. The more familiar you are with all the details the better. Some time ago at a service, I had finished the eulogy before I realized that there was no casket behind me as I had been talking. It was only a memorial service. If you are holding the service at the mortuary, the director will usually direct you to a clergyperson's study where you can wait and meditate until it is time for the service to begin. Someone will get you when it is time to start and usher you to take your place.

I try to have firmly impressed on my mind the order of service, that is, when I will read, when I will pray, and when hymns will be sung or played. You can also, if you have not already done so, mark the Scriptures you will be using so you will have ready access to them. Read over your obituary notes carefully.

MAKE COPIES

Have your secretary prepare copies of the order of service for you, the mortician, the soloist, the organist, and anyone else involved with the service. It will save time and embarrassing moments of uncertainty. Leave nothing to chance. If the funeral director is to close the service, it will help him or her to know how you will end the eulogy (directors do not always listen during the eulogy).

I also like to number the survivors on my notes so I will not miss them as I read the obituary, as in the following:

1. wife
2. first son
3. second son
4. first daughter
5. second daughter
6. fourteen grandchildren

Obviously, I don't read these aloud; the numbering helps me to keep in proper sequence so I don't forget anyone.

OVERCOME YOUR JITTERS

After four decades of conducting services, I still get nervous. But there are three basic and necessary ways to overcome nervousness as you wait for the service to begin.

1. Pray. Pray for God's wisdom, his strength, his consolation for the family. Pray often and pray boldly.

2. Prepare. You should always be prepared fully. If you are a novice you may wonder if there is such a thing as being fully prepared. The answer, of course, is relative, but you should by the time of the service have your eulogy fully written and you should have gone over it, rehearsing it several times so that you are comfortable with your notes.

3. Breathe out deeply several times. The idea is not to take deep breaths but to expel all the air from your lungs several times. This will have a calming effect on you.

REASSURE THE FAMILY

Your confidence will help them and will help you, too. It will have the additional benefit of getting your mind off yourself.

IF YOU MAKE A MISTAKE

If you commit a blunder, correct it quickly and go on. Once during a funeral, the order of service called for me to read a selection from Scripture and then to lead a prayer. I read the Scripture and had stepped off the raised platform before I remembered that I was to lead the prayer (I had not checked my own order of service). Trying to think quickly, I decided I should lead the prayer from where I was standing. I was able to do that all right, but I committed another blunder that was even worse. I said something like, "Lord, we are all here prostate before you." I quickly corrected it to *prostrate.* Amazingly, no one caught it or made an issue of it.

SPEAK TO THE FAMILY DIRECTLY

While attending a funeral of a Jewish friend some years ago, my wife and I were impressed by the rabbi's delivery. One of his strengths was the firm eye contact that he continually made with the family and, to a lesser degree, with all of us. In any conversation it is important to make honest eye contact with your listeners. Be sure to talk with the family and mourners during your eulogy in this way.

BE HONEST

A eulogy should not be a performance. It is not a place for theatrical or dramatic effects. You are there as a representative of the Lord and as a friend of the family. It is your purpose to help the mourners confront the reality of death, to come to terms with their loss, and to be confronted with God's love and his claim on our lives.

STAND BY THE CASKET WHEN YOU ARE FINISHED

When you have concluded your part of the service, whether by prayer or not, walk to the casket and stand at the foot. If someone is assisting you in the service, he or she can stand at one end of the casket and you at the other.

This usually serves as a signal to the director that you have finished. At this point the director will come forward to direct the mourners so they can pass by the casket, view the remains to pay their respects, and then go to the grave site. Remain by the casket until the mourners have passed by.

Once the visitors are gone, the family is usually given an opportunity to see the deceased one more time. I have found it best to step back out of the way, but to watch for any family member who has a special need. This often will be the most emotional part of the service. If someone is especially hurting or grief stricken, you can put a hand on that person's shoulder to demonstrate your concern and support. Grievers should not be made to feel rushed.

Chapter Nine

IMPORTANT MISCELLANY

CHARGING FOR YOUR SERVICES

In some religious persuasions it is customary to charge a fee for your services. After all, don't all other professional persons receive remuneration for their expertise? On the other hand, most ministers are paid by their churches. Should they charge church members for doing church work on church time?

I have had minister friends who do not accept any honoraria. I have heard of ministers and persons of the cloth who charge what I regard as exorbitant fees for their services.

My course has been never to charge a fee for a funeral. If you deal with a mortuary, it will usually be collected by them and then given to you by check on the day of the service. If the deceased was a member of your church, the mortuary will sometimes ask the family if they wish to pay you directly. Usually the funeral director will let you know of the family's decision. Frequently the family will offer you an envelope on the day of the service. At times they will pay you when you make your follow-up call on the home. When it is offered, I accept it with a warm thank you and state that it was not necessary. I have had a few families not offer anything — not even a thank you — but they have been very few.

In cases where the family was in hardship I have told them beforehand that I wanted nothing and have returned it when they offered.

I have always believed that God will reward me if I do his will first and put money second. He is always faithful.

MAKING FOLLOW-UP CALLS

When you leave the family on the day of the funeral, you can propose your calling on them in a few days. I try to make that call within three to seven days of the service. What is the purpose? To see how the family members are doing. Sometimes they have a real letdown after all the out-of-town family members leave and after the initial rush of attention diminishes.

They should be encouraged to continue their quiet reflection. You can encourage church members to spend time with them. It is a great time for ministry. Grievers are often more amenable to the word of God at this time in their lives than at any other.

But make sure they understand that your intentions are honorable, not amorous. If you are calling on a person of the opposite sex, take an older, sincere believer of the opposite sex with you so no misunderstandings can develop. Many years ago I believe I made a young woman uncomfortable by my offer to call on her later, even though I explained completely what my purpose was. And by calling on one older woman more than once, I created an extremely awkward situation for myself. She was forty years older than I and completely unattractive to me, but apparently because of her background she had only one interpretation of any interest shown in her. It's best to train church members to make follow-up calls on grievers and have them take over after the initial visit.

DEALING WITH FRATERNAL ORDERS

There are many persons in this country who belong to lodges and fraternal organizations. Most of these groups have a funeral ritual for their members. In some cases they will handle the whole service. In other cases the deceased or the deceased's family desires you to cooperate with the lodge members.

Some ministers refuse to cooperate with fraternal orders. You will have to decide on the basis of your conscience. It would help you to investigate the meaning of the service that they perform. In some instances the ritual has secret or hidden meaning that members must not reveal.

I have cooperated with them, but I always insist that they complete their rituals before I begin. That way it is understood that what I say has no relationship with lodge ritual. Then I do my best to divorce the minds of the hearers from the previous ritual. This is the only way that I can conscientiously participate.

AIDS

In recent years AIDS, a problem unforeseen over the past centuries, has developed into a major concern. It has increasing complications and implications. Two questions are, what are the health risks of people at the service who may touch the deceased, and how should a minister direct his comments?

At the time of this writing the medical profession tells us that risk is only through transfer of blood or body fluids, so I don't feel there is a great risk in the touch factor. Far more difficult for me has been what to say. I have done several services of persons who have died of AIDS. I frankly don't feel that a person who has contracted AIDS through homosexual activity is different in death from a miser, adulterer, gossip, or anyone whose life is not in order with God.

Only a person whose life is right with God has any hope, according to my convictions. We can never be sure where a person's heart is. In a few of those cases of AIDS victims there was sincere repentance before God. I believe that God forgives them.

If you will note the sample eulogies I have included, I never say with confidence anyone is going to heaven or hell, because I don't know a person's heart and mind. Only God knows that (see 1 Corinthians 4:1-5). But I am convinced that one must be right with God to see him.

DEALING WITH CONFLICT

Occasionally family conflicts will erupt. Often you become aware of them as you meet with the family to make arrangements. At times the grievers will speak of some estranged family member no one has seen; no one knows for sure whether he will appear or how he will behave. As the incidence of divorce increases, there will be more situations of possible conflict among stepfamily members.

I have found it helpful to talk with the family beforehand as to the possibility of conflict. If they bring up the subject, I review with them options for dealing with it. The options I suggest are along the lines of understanding and forgiveness.

Sometimes situations develop you are not prepared for. Many years ago at the close of a service, the wife and mother of the deceased argued over who would see him last before the casket was closed.

There are some rules of thumb I try to follow in these situations.

1. I try to get all parties to work toward compromise.

2. In the case of a minor, the parents' wishes should prevail. If it is a divided family, it should be the wishes of the parent who has custody of the child.

3. The wishes of the deceased expressed in his or her will should be carried out.

4. The wife's or husband's desire should be carried out before the parents', regardless of the age of the deceased.

5. In the case of Christians, I try to get them to go the second mile in showing compassion and understanding in their relationships with non-Christians. I see this as a good opportunity for Christians to demonstrate God's love.

6. If your conscience is compromised in any way, you can politely step aside and courteously request that someone else not affected as you are conduct the service.

7. In all cases I believe I must be true to the Word of God as I understand it. His will must prevail in all I do.

OPEN OR CLOSED CASKETS?

The "case is closed" by most people on the subject of viewing remains at services. Family members will often insist, "I want to remember Daddy as he was alive, not dead." The argument seems compelling and logical. If family members who are arranging the service are insistent enough, you will have no option. The casket will be closed. Others believe the casket should not be left open for other reasons. "Mom is not there," they may say. Or, "it is pagan to look at a corpse."

Probably the real issue for these people is that they are terrified of death. Over the years I've been interested in the body language of mourners who pass by the casket at the close of the service. Some will approach the casket directly, linger to sob, touch the corpse, and say their goodbyes. Others will make a sharp turn away from the casket as soon as they see the side exit. Fear of death at viewing time can almost be measured in feet and inches.

Some people have left prior instructions saying they want no viewing of their bodies when they are gone.

If you are a novice in the ministry or are new in your area of service, investigate the regional, cultural, and religious customs.

In many cases, the family will ask your opinion regarding viewing. Whether you are undecided or decided, you may want to consider another perspective on viewing remains. One of your purposes as a minister is to help people confront death. Viewing remains is a healthy step in the direction of confrontation. What the mourner must come to terms with is the finality of death. Seeing the loved one in the casket helps this to happen much sooner and more completely.

I believe it is very helpful for all concerned to have the casket open before or after the service. Whether it should be open during the service may be best decided by your own style of delivering eulogies. If you want people to hear your message in any context, you will want as few distractions as possible — visual, audible, or otherwise. You will already be competing with flowers, latecomers, and assorted sniffling and coughing (and even singing birds that some morticians enclose in their chapels). Fixing on the sight of the corpse may be an overpowering urge from which you will not be able to free some mourners.

On the other hand, I've seen some priests and ministers stand directly by an open casket and talk about the departed one very effectively. The choice here should be made according to your style.

Chapter Ten

SAMPLE EULOGIES

In some cases names and a few details in these sample eulogies are changed for the sake of privacy. I have followed the format outlined earlier in the book.

SAMPLE EULOGY 1

This eulogy was given at the service of a man who died in middle age. His death was a result of the lifestyle he had followed most of his adult life. However, he made a serious commitment to God in his last days.

Text: Ephesians 2:4-9

Comments

It might seem contradictory to you to talk of God's love in the presence of death. His love seems remote. Suffering and death have prevailed again. It is true, as Shakespeare said, "We are cabined, cribbed, confined."

As was observed in the *Rubáiyát of Omar Khayyám*, "Strange — is it not? — that of the myriads who before us passed the door of darkness through, not one returns to tell us of the road, which we discover we must travel, too." We all lose this great conflict, this terrible struggle with death.

Death has many opening scenarios. A chest pain turning into a massive heart failure; the screeching and crushing of cars at an intersection; the sudden violent quakes of the earth; the lost memory of Alzheimer's; the hard-fought battle against a raging disease — all of these are death's opening scenes. They are varied, but the stillness of death's final scene is always the same. Death always wins.

The great conflict of life and death transcends the human realm. That's one of the first things the Bible tells us.

God's creation is good and beautiful. But that goodness can be maintained only by serving and pleasing our Creator.

Our first ancestors believed the good was in possessions and enlightenment. They desired that fruit passionately. It deceived them as it deceives us. We spend our lives needing acceptance and love and understanding.

We allow ourselves to be deceived into thinking our possessions, power, and intelligence will fill that void within us. But they only make us more distant, alone, alienated.

As Cesare Borgia lamented, "I have provided in the course of my life for everything except death; and now, alas! I am to die entirely unprepared."

What can we do to prepare ourselves? How do we face this grisly foe? How do we deal with this awesome enemy? There are definite steps to victory.

First, we must admit, acknowledge — concede — how dreadfully death affects us, how mightily it controls us, how it haunts us in the night, stalks the recesses of our minds, assaults our tranquility.

Second, we must confess our own sin. John wrote in 1 John 1:9: "If we confess our sins, [God] is faithful and just and will forgive us our sins and purify us from all unrighteousness."

Third, when we lose a loved one, as we have today, we should spend time reflecting, remembering, reviewing.

John, Jewel, Ann, Marlene, there are, no doubt, vivid recollections of Bill's childhood or yours in Kansas. Perhaps it will center on Bill's love for classical music and the piano, his enormous compassion and kindness for you and his friends.

(Here I read a story about Bill's childhood given me by his sister.)

I first met Bill about thirty years ago and was always impressed by his gentlemanly, upbeat spirit, his sense of fairness and his concern for others. Bill was gifted, artistic, was a successful wigmaker and stylist. He made the elderly look younger and helped those undergoing chemotherapy to restore their dignity.

In the world, among people, Bill was successful and was loved by nearly everyone. But many of the things we tend to value in varying degrees were extremely important to him.

He loved silver; was possessed by it.

He was always meticulous about his appearance.

He also followed a lifestyle advocated by the world.

He allowed himself to be deceived by lust of the eyes, lust of flesh, and pride of life.

As our text in Ephesians said, "All of us also lived among them at one time, gratifying the cravings of our sinful nature and following its desires and thoughts." He was "dead in transgressions."

As Ann mentioned, "Bill grew up in a home where he heard about Jesus but never really came to know him, that is, until the last three months of his life." Then he fell in love with God. Bill came to understand the deceitfulness of possessions and position. Ann noted, "His desire for material possessions peeled off like layers of old paint."

That meticulous desire for an unblemished physical appearance was discarded. Though he knew his condition was likely terminal, he wanted you his friends and others to know about Jesus, to turn from vanity and carnal ways.

When Bill first learned of his condition, he responded by saying, "I'm not afraid. If this is what it takes for God to get my attention, I'm glad." He firmly believed these statements from Scripture:

If anyone is in Christ, he is a new creation; the old has gone (2 Corinthians 5:17).

But because of his great love for us, God, who is rich in mercy, made us alive with Christ even when we were dead in transgressions —

it is by grace you have been saved. And God raised us up with Christ and seated us with him in the heavenly realms in Christ Jesus, in order that in the coming ages he might show the incomparable riches of his grace, expressed in his kindness to us in Christ Jesus. For it is by grace you have been saved, through faith — and this not . . . by works, so that no one can boast (Ephesians 2:4-9).

Bill came to understand God's grace in many ways. First, he knew that we are saved by grace, not by works. Romans 8:1 says: "Therefore, there is now no condemnation for those who are in Christ Jesus." What a wonderful feeling to know that God has saved us by his mercy; it is not earned or purchased or bought. It is paid for fully by the sacrifice of Jesus.

Second, as the writer of Hebrews declared, God has said: "Never will I leave you; never will I forsake you" (Hebrews 13:5). Bill's physical condition required almost constant attention over the past several weeks, and the Lord provided a team. It consisted of Larry, his long-time friend, whom God helped overcome disease in his life so that he could be available; Ann, who was able to help over the summertime and also utilized vacation time; Constance, who had been hospitalized because of severe struggles, but functioned beautifully to assist. All three felt privileged to serve Bill. His dear friend, Francine, called daily with words of encouragement and love.

God did not forsake Bill. In fact, Bill rejoiced in Christ each day. The words of Paul to the Philippians encouraged him:

Do not be anxious about anything, but in everything, by prayer and petition, with thanksgiving, present your requests to God. And the peace of God, which transcends all understanding, will guard your hearts and your minds in Christ Jesus (Philippians 4:6, 7).

Jesus urged his disciples not to fret or to be fearful: "Do not let your hearts be troubled. Trust in God; trust also in me. In my father's house are many rooms" (John 14:1).

How could Jesus say this? (1) He is God's one and only Son. He lived a perfect life and was tempted in every way, as we are, yet without sinning. (2) He was everything the prophets said in Scriptures he should be: born in Bethlehem, reared in Nazareth, and pierced for our transgressions. (3) He was crucified for our failure. (4) God raised him on the third day. According to 1 Corinthians 15 he was seen by more than five hundred witnesses at one time. (5) Jesus is now at God's right hand.

God gives us this promise: If we will turn away from our vain quests and empty pursuits, our pride, and turn to him — to belief in his Son, Jesus — God grants us victory over death.

> Listen, I tell you a mystery: We will not all sleep, but we will all be changed — in a flash, in the twinkling of an eye, at the last trumpet. For the trumpet will sound, the dead will be raised imperishable, and we will be changed. For the perishable must clothe itself with the imperishable, and the mortal with immortality. When the perishable has been clothed with the imperishable, and the mortal with immortality, then the saying that is written will come true: "Death has been swallowed up in victory" (1 Corinthians 15:51-54).

The promise of resurrection, I know, sounds unbelievable to modern minds. It was just as incredible to ancient people. In response, I'd like to tell a story I read some years ago.

Many years ago a boy spent the day fishing on the banks of the Mississippi. The fishing was not good that day, but there was an old man fishing nearby, and the two began to chat. Their conversation went on amiably until dusk, when a sternwheeler could be seen off in the distance plying up the river. As soon as the boy saw the river boat, he began to jump up and down. Pulling his red handkerchief from his hip pocket, he waved it, hoping to catch the attention of someone on the boat. Observing the boy's behavior, the old man chided his younger companion, "Son, what you are doing is stupid. No boat like that is going to stop for a little boy." The old man went back to his fishing. He looked up later to see that the boat was actually slowing down and approaching the bank where they were standing. A gangplank was lowered, and the little boy excitedly jumped on board to hugs from the crew. But he turned back to the old man, remonstrating, "I'm not stupid, Mister. My daddy is the captain of this riverboat, and we're on our way to a new home upriver."

In the same way, we believe that Jesus is the captain of our salvation and will gladly come back for us to take us to our new home in heaven.

SAMPLE EULOGY 2

This eulogy was given at the graveside of a boy about two years old. He died after prolonged suffering from congenital problems.

Text: *Matthew 19:13, 14*

Comments

We have come to share with Charles and Linda and their families in the loss of Eric. We have come to weep with them, to feel with them the keen sense of separation, to wonder in anguish, to ask for understanding and forgiveness from our mutual Father, God, to share in a profoundly painful and vexing moment.

We do not come today with any glib answers. Our hearts are shattered as we stand here in grief. To see life cut so extremely short is stressful and difficult to understand. We can't help thinking what might have been. At this, anger and frustration well up within us.

Though I believe that God would prefer that we honestly express our anguish, verbalize our fears, and speak of the hopes now dashed, there is one thing we must not do. We cannot let guilt overwhelm us or divide us in our love for one another. We need to openly express our feelings of guilt for our past behaviors so God's healing can take place. As the apostle John instructed, "If we confess our sins, [God] is faithful and just and will forgive us our sins and purify us from all unrighteousness" (1 John 1:9). We want Charles and Linda to know of our love and support for them.

One thing we all must do is positively affirm the constant care of God. Jesus personified that love as he blessed and prayed for the children brought to him. It is instructive that Jesus' concern and love for little children rose up in spite of the mire of selfishness and calloused ambition of adults.

God also proved, beyond all human questionings and doubts, his love for us through his own suffering and anguish. He stood by and watched as his only Son's life was taken from him. Though God could have acted to save Jesus, he did not do so, to show that even at the pinnacle of man's wickedness, God's love and forgiving nature could be displayed for all time. We have the assurance of God's care. As Jesus declared, "I give them eternal life, and they shall never perish; no one can snatch them out of my hand" (John 10:28).

I am confident that Charles and Linda feel that expectancy of David. When the infant son born of Bathsheba died, David was well aware of the fixed manner of life and death, as seen in his question: "Can I bring him back again?" Though David knew that was impossible, he did express a great hope and expectancy: "I will go to him, but he will not return to me" (2 Samuel 12:23). We believe that Eric is safe in the hands of God, and that Charles and Linda, and all of us, can go to be with him.

The book of Revelation describes that hope for which we long:

> Then I saw a new heaven and a new earth, for the first heaven and the first earth had passed away, and there was no longer any sea. I saw the Holy City, the new Jerusalem, coming down out of heaven from God, prepared as a bride beautifully dressed for her husband. And I heard a loud voice from the throne saying, "Now the dwelling of God is with men, and he will live with them. They will be his people, and God himself will be with them and be their God. He will wipe every tear from their eyes. There will be no more death or mourning or crying or pain, for the old order of things has passed away" (Revelation 21:1-4).

SAMPLE EULOGY 3

This service was prepared for a woman in her late seventies who died as she was preparing to move out of state to live with her daughter. She had been a church member for about five years.

Text: Romans 8:38, 39

Comments

This is one of the most sublime and assuring promises ever made. The source of it is God himself who promises that no power can separate one of his children from him. No power on earth or heaven, no power of the present or the future can affect the one trusting in Jesus.

It is not by accident that Paul mentioned death first in the order of all the threats that interfere with our relationship with God. It is in the presence of death that we feel most alone, most threatened, most fearful and anxious. Death strikes us all. It usually leaves the survivors pervaded with guilt and terror. The prophet Isaiah aptly described death as "the covering that is cast over all peoples, the veil that is spread over all nations. . . . the reproach of his people" (Isaiah 25:7, 8, RSV).

Paul defined it as the last enemy to be destroyed. Because death is inextricably bound up with our sin and is the wages of sin, it is awesome and fearsome. It is unremitting. We come today to admit its power and the hold it has over all flesh.

We feel the stark contrast between a few days ago when Emma was so vibrant, so alive, so filled with expectancy, and the present silence and solicitude. Our remembrances of Emma are images of her energetic approach to life. There was no blandness in her. She dressed colorfully, expressed herself vividly, and was always vivacious.

Emma was a trained dietician. She majored in home economics at the university and always had a creative interest in food and nutrition. Her neighbors enjoyed the tastes and aromas of her homemade pies and cakes.

Emma had an active, indomitable spirit. She worked hard to help Susan get through college. She was employed by [company name] and later by [company name], where she was a valuable part of the corporation. She applied the same sense of industry and organization during her preparations to move in the past few months. A caring, giving person, she loved people. By the testimony of her family she was also "a great baby-sitter."

Susan and her family were the great love of Emma's life. She spoke often of them and always proudly. Susan is thankful for the strong, loving relationship her mother and she had from earliest times. Emma held her son-in-law in greatest esteem and spoke proudly of her grandchildren. What vivid recollections we all shall always possess of the broad, warm smile and the brightness of her eyes! We treasure them.

Emma was not perfect. Our grief has not occluded her foibles, nor do we desire that. She could speak with a resolute directness that caused you to cower. But it is the faults and weaknesses she had and that we all possess, most of us to a greater degree than Emma, that make us understand that we all need help.

We were all placed on this earth by our Creator to praise him, to love and honor all of his other creatures and creation. We have failed miserably in God's intention for us. He is holy and good. In contrast, we often choose lifestyles, thought patterns, and ambitions that separate us from God. We are involved with sin and death. That's why Jesus came from God: to show us the beauty of a lifestyle of love — a love so true and firmly fixed that he voluntarily died to pay the penalty of our failure.

Then came the most marvelous miracle of history: he was alive again three days later. It is a fact witnessed by five hundred persons at one time. Where is Jesus now? At the right hand of God pleading, interceding with the Father for those who trust and believe him. The writer of Hebrews made reference to what we have just related: first, our responsibility to God; second, our need of the help offered in his Son; third, the willingness and the ability he has to help us. The New Testament assures us: "Nothing in all creation is hidden from God's sight. Everything is uncovered and laid bare before the eyes of him to whom we must give account" (Hebrews 4:13).

> Therefore, since we have a great high priest who has gone through the heavens, Jesus the Son of God, let us hold firmly to the faith we profess. For we do not have a high priest who is unable to sympathize with our weaknesses, but we have one who has been tempted in every way, just as we are — yet was without sin. Let us then approach the throne of grace with confidence, so that we may receive mercy and find grace to help us in our time of need (see Hebrews 4:14-16).

I said earlier that the two things most common in the presence of death are guilt and terror. We don't have to approach this day with dread and apprehension. Praise God that both guilt and terror are removed by the presence of Jesus who holds us permanently in the Father.

Because he died to pay the penalty of our guilt, forgiveness is available to those who will claim it. The apostle John promised: "If we confess our sins, God is faithful and just and will forgive us our sins and purify us from all unrighteousness" (1 John 1:9).

Though fear of death keeps many of us in bondage, even death's terror has been removed. Jesus destroyed him who has the power over death. We can join him in his resurrection. Thank God, Emma shared that hope. She came to know her Lord and Creator in recent years, studied with many of us on Thursdays, and was maturing in him.

What a difference it makes when we are prepared for this day in Christ because we know that "neither death nor life, neither angels nor demons, neither the present nor the future, nor any powers, neither height nor depth, nor anything else in all creation, will be able to separate us from the love of God that is in Christ Jesus our Lord" (Romans 8:38-39).

We shall close with the great resurrection assurance Paul wrote to those grieving Greeks centuries ago:

> Brothers, we do not want you to be ignorant about those who fall asleep, or to grieve like the rest of men, who have no hope. We believe that Jesus died and rose again and so we believe that God will bring with Jesus those who have fallen asleep in him. According to the Lord's own word, we tell you that we who are still alive, who are left till the coming of the Lord, will certainly not precede those who have fallen asleep. For the Lord himself will come down from heaven, with a loud command, with the voice of the archangel and with the trumpet call of God, and the dead in Christ will rise first. After that, we who are still alive and are left will be caught up together with them in the clouds to meet the Lord in the air. And so we will be with the Lord forever. Therefore encourage each other with these words (1 Thessalonians 4:13-18).

SAMPLE EULOGY 4

This eulogy was delivered at the service for a woman in her eighties who had been a long-time member of the church and had taught Sunday school for many years.

Text: *1 Thessalonians 4:13-18*

Comments

We are gathered to pay our respects to Esta, to grieve for her, but to also exult in the victory of our Savior.

(Following the obituary, stating birth, marriage, and survivors, I continued.) She had been a teacher in Northern California and Nevada and then taught for several years at Pacific Christian Academy in Graton, California.

She and her husband, along with her brother and his wife, were instrumental in starting the Church of Christ in Sebastopol, California, about 1948. They constructed the building literally by hand. We want to review Esta's life more at length.

Esta's longtime friend, whose three children were all taught by her, will lead us in two hymns: "Safe in the Arms of Jesus," and "The New Song." Following that, our associate minister will read Psalm 23. An elder of the church, whose four children were all taught by Esta, will direct us in prayer.

(Following this, I began the eulogy.)

"His loved ones are very precious to him and he does not lightly let them die" (Psalm 116:15, LB).

Esta had marked this verse in her Living Bible, the verse that is rendered by many translations: "Precious in the sight of the LORD is the death of his saints."

The awareness of our finiteness, of the brevity and frailty of our lives, haunts us. Every generation since Adam has been anxious. We are, "through fear of death, subject to lifelong bondage." Life is tenuous, fragile. It is unpredictable. It often takes sudden turns that find us unprepared.

To unbelievers there seems a randomness about life wherein there is fortune or misfortune depending on nothing more meaningful than the flip of a coin or the throw of the dice. There are those who have good runs of chance, but at some point one's luck must run out.

Even believers, those whose faith is strong, look askance at the events of life. They are aware of God's presence and power. They know his creative activity. For them the crucial question is: Does God care about what happens to us? Does he forget our personal needs, our fears, our wants, our need for his presence?

Thus David himself began Psalm 13 wrestling with those vexing questions that wrench and strain the minds of believers: "How long, O LORD? Will you forget me forever? How long will you hide your face from me? How long must I wrestle with my thoughts and every day have sorrow in my heart? . . . Look on me and answer, O LORD my God."

The difficulty we have understanding God's ways can be stated no more forthrightly than by a young lad who reasoned, "I don't think God is fair. He lets us die. But he doesn't die himself."

It is because this young man's two main premises were misguided that he came to the wrong conclusion about God's fairness. God does not desire our death. Neither does he sit by idly while we die.

Esta knew well the truth of that. That's why she marked the passage, "His loved ones are very precious to him and he does not lightly let them die," in her Bible.

Helen Keller once noted: "Unless we form the habit of going to the Bible in bright moments as well as in trouble, we cannot fully respond to its consolations because we lack equilibrium between light and darkness."

Few people have ever achieved that balance of Bible knowledge, but Esta did.

Esta had numerous talents: her creativity expressed itself in many ways. She loved to write, to paint, to sew. She made many of her daughter's clothes. She loved to entertain, to cook. She was famous for her homemade bread and boysenberry cobbler. As her brother, George, commented, "There were not enough hours for her in a day."

Her greatest desire for others was for them to see what God has done for the world in Christ. She had a special gift for enabling and motivating young people to comprehend the truth of Scripture.

She heartily agreed with Samuel Chadwick's observation that "no man is uneducated who knows the Bible, and no one is wise who is ignorant of its teachings."

One of the most significant things she did was to put together a book on Christ in the Old Testament, researching and assembling information given her by her uncle. It is a marvelous review of symbols and prophecies of Christ found throughout the Old Testament prophets.

It was at Esta's behest that I began writing lessons on the Old Testament predictions of the Messiah and their fulfillment. It has launched me on a lifelong project.

She deeply respected God's Word. She instilled that respect in her students. To Esta the promises of God were vibrantly alive. Those who studied under her were impressed by God's influence and power.

The gift of teaching did not come easily to Esta. She gave arduous hours to study and to perfecting her teaching skills. She committed much Scripture to memory and demanded that her students do the same. She gave them lessons that required considerable homework and preparation. They were not disdainful or scornful of her demands. Instead, they esteemed her and came to reverence the Word.

My wife and I are thankful that all of our children were able to study under her. Every parent I have ever known here has shared that same joy. She continued to teach and inspire until well into her eighty-first year.

In her final illness she received many calls and notes from former students. One young man wrote:

Dear Esta:

How I love you for teaching me about God; for fueling the spark that lit this soul on fire; for making classes fun and learning simple.

But most of all I love you for showing me our Father's love through your life and actions. Things that cannot be taught in class — the never-ending lesson of life and love — you have shown to me and is forever living in my soul.

Love that endures forever.

Steve

One young woman wrote:

Dear Esta:

I just wanted to tell you I've been thinking of you and hope you feel a lot better. I hope to see you soon. If I don't come in time, I'll surely see you in heaven!

I love you lots!!

Love, Kari

P.S. Thank you for teaching me to be a Christian. I'm holding you up in my prayers.

Esta's own daughter and son know well the beauty of their mother's devotion to them, the strength of her faith.

Esta was not perfect. The only perfection she would ever have claimed is the perfection of God's love in Christ.

But there was an unwavering hope in her that "God's loved ones are very precious to him and he does not lightly let them die."

The confidence she had in our Lord was resolute even to her death.

Rare is that one who along with Paul would say, "For to me to live is Christ, and to die is gain. . . . that with full courage now as always Christ will be honored in my body, whether by life or by death" (Philippians 1:21, 20, RSV).

During many recent Sundays large groups would gather around Esta's bed to sing hymns of faith, read Scripture, pray, and share communion with her. She knew she was in her last days. But as the Scriptures were read and as hymns were sung, she had what can be described best as a beatific visage, "as though it were the face of an angel."

Her trust has made a lasting impact. One longtime friend wrote Esta's daughter: "May you find comfort in knowing what a beautiful legacy your mother left. She touched my life, as one of many, and made me a better person. She will live in my heart always."

Esta would insist, of course, that it is all from the Lord who made heaven and earth. The passage she asked to be read most often in her final days was Romans 8. Some selected verses from the great chapter (Romans 8:28-39) affirm the joy and beauty of a life that trusts in Christ.

What was the foundation of Esta's hope? It is that God does not take lightly either our sin or our death. She was awed by the implications of 2 Corinthians 5:21: "God made him who had no sin to be sin for us, so that in him we might become the righteousness of God."

Jesus died to put away our sin from us. We are precious to him. And he was raised to show that God does not take our death lightly, either.

> So will it be with the resurrection of the dead. The body that is sown is perishable, it is raised imperishable; it is sown in dishonor, it is raised in glory; it is sown in weakness, it is raised in power; it is sown a natural body, it is raised a spiritual body (1 Corinthians 15:42-44).

> Listen, I tell you a mystery: We will not all sleep, but we will all be changed — in a flash, in the twinkling of an eye, at the last trumpet. For the trumpet will sound, the dead will be raised imperishable, and we will be changed. For the perishable must clothe itself with the imperishable, and the mortal with immortality. When the perishable has been clothed with the imperishable, and the mortal with immortality, then the saying that is written will come true: "Death has been swallowed up in victory" (1 Corinthians 15:51-54).

> Therefore, my dear brothers, stand firm. Let nothing move you. Always give yourselves fully to the work of the Lord, because you know that your labor is not in vain (1 Corinthians 15:58).

How to Use The Resources Section

In Part 2 of the book you will find Scriptures, poems, hymns, and a sample committal prayer.

The Scriptures are indexed by subject. An index of poems by subject is followed by the poems in alphabetical order by title. Some of the poems are too long to read in their entirety. They are included because you may find some lines to fit your particular situation. For example, see "On an Infant Dying as Soon as Born," pages 108-110, lines 29 and 30: "The stern-eyed fate descry, that babe or mother, one must die." You may have to give a eulogy for an infant whose death was due to the above circumstance. It is probably unwise to attempt reading more than eight to ten lines at once.

Hymns are listed alphabetically, preceded by suggestions for use.

Following a sample committal prayer are a few poems based on Scripture to accompany your prayer and Scripture at graveside or niche side.

Chapter Eleven

SCRIPTURES
BY SUBJECT

When whole chapters are listed, I'm indicating that most of the verses in the chapter are helpful. However, it is probably wise to use selected verses and to avoid lengthy readings.

Adversity, patience in	James 5:7-11
Age and youth	Ecclesiastes 12:1
Appeal for God to hear	Psalm 119:169
Appeal for God's care	Psalm 17:6-8
Appeal for God's mercy	Jeremiah 10:23, 24
	Habakkuk 3:2
Appeal for mercy	Psalm 6
Appeal for relief	Psalm 4
Appeal to God for help	Psalm 121
Atoning sacrifice of Jesus	1 John 2:12
Believers, confidence of	1 John 5:13-15
Benediction	1 Peter 5:10,11
	Hebrews 13:20, 21
	Jude 24, 25
Blessed are the dead in Christ	Revelation 14:13
Blessing	Numbers 6:24-26
	2 Corinthians 13:14
Book of Life	Daniel 12:1-3
	Revelation 20:11-15

Brevity of life	Psalm 39:1-7
	James 4:13-17
Brevity and uncertainty of life	Job 16:18-22
	Job 17:1-11
Children, God's care for	Matthew 18:1-3
	Matthew 18:10-14
	Mark 10:13-16
Christ, hope in	1 Thessalonians 4:13-18
Christ's saving work	Hebrews 2:5-18
Comfort for the weary	Isaiah 40:28-31
Comfort in suffering	2 Corinthians 1:3, 4
Confidence in God's care	Psalm 23:6
Confidence in obedience	1 John 3:21-24
Confidence of believers	1 John 5:13-15
Confidence of faithful life	2 Timothy 4:1-8
Consolation	Matthew 11:28-30
Day of the Lord described	2 Peter 3:10-13
Dead in Christ blessed	Revelation 14:13
Death defeated	Isaiah 25:6-9
Death of infant	Isaiah 65:20
Death, man forsaken	Psalm 22:15
Death, no ransom for	Psalm 49:7-9
	Psalm 49:12-14
Death, preparing for	1 Peter 4:7-11
Death, need to prepare for	Luke 12:16-21
Death and judgment, need to prepare for	1 Thessalonians 5:4-11
	Titus 2:11-14
	Hebrews 3:12-15
Death's threat	Psalm 18:1-6
Distress	Psalm 102:23-28
	Psalm 4
Earthquake, death from	Psalm 60:1-5
Eternal life, certainty of	2 Samuel 12:13-23
Eternal nature of God	Hebrews 1:10-12
Expressions of desolation	Psalm 77:1-12
Faith, description and example	Hebrews 11:1-40
Faith, lack of	Luke 8:22-25

God's wisdom	Romans 11:33-36
Good life rewarded	Matthew 25:31-46
Greatness and sovereignty of God	Psalm 8
Guilt, help with	Psalm 32:1-7
Healing after tragedy	Hosea 6:1-3
Heaven as goal	Philippians 3:12-14
	Philippians 3:20-21
	Colossians 3:1-4
Heaven described	Isaiah 65:17-25
	Revelation 21:1-5
	Revelation 21:10-27
Heaven's glory described	Revelation 7:9-17
Heaven's praise and rejoicing	Revelation 19:4-10
Help in dealing with guilt	Psalm 32:1-7
Hiddenness of God	Psalm 102:1-3
	Habakkuk 1:2-4
Hope in Christ	1 Thessalonians 4:13-18
Hope in righteousness	Psalm 37:18
Hope in suffering	Romans 5:1-5
Infant death	Isaiah 65:20
Jesus, atoning sacrifice of	1 John 2:1, 2
Jesus, first and last	Revelation 22:13
Judgment (*also see* Death and judgment)	Revelation 22:12
Judgment, certainty of	Hebrews 9:26b-28
Justice of God	Psalm 11
Keys of death, Christ holding	Revelation 1:12-18
Lack of faith	Luke 8:22-25
Love defined	1 Corinthians 13:1-13
Love of God	Psalm 63:1-8
	Romans 8:31-39
Life, book of	Daniel 12:1-3
Life, brevity of	Psalm 39:1-7
	James 4:13-17
Life, brevity and uncertainty	Job 17:1-11
Life, of few days and full of trouble	Job 14:1-14
Life, tree of	Revelation 22:14

Life, tree of and river of	Revelation 22:1-5
Man forsaken in death	Psalm 22:1-5
Man's helplessness before God*	Job 4:7-21
Man's helplessness in death	Job 1:21
Men born to trouble*	Job 5:7-11
Men like grass	1 Peter 1:22-25
Mercy, appeal for	Psalm 6
Mercy of God	Jonah 2:1-9
Mercy, plea for	Psalm 51:1-12
Mother and wife	Proverbs 31:10-31
Mourning, example of	2 Samuel 1:11-27
	Acts 9:32-42
Nearness of God	Psalm 145:18
Obedience, confidence in	1 John 3:21-24
Old age described metaphorically	Ecclesiastes 12
Patience in adversity	James 5:7-11
Plea for mercy	Psalm 51:1-12
Plea of a dying man	Psalm 88
Praise God for greatness	Psalm 103:1-5
	Psalm 103:8-22
Preparing for death and judgment	1 Thessalonians 5:4-11
	Titus 2:11-14
	Hebrews 3:12-15
Preparing for death, need for	Luke 12:16-21
Promise of Christ to one who overcomes	Revelation 2:7
	Revelation 2:11
	Revelation 2:17
	Revelation 2:26-29
	Revelation 3:5
	Revelation 3:12
	Revelation 3:21
Raising of young man (Eutychus)	Acts 20:7-12

---

*Though there are some good observations in these texts and they are often used in funerals, as you will notice, they are the words of Eliphaz the Temanite. God was not too pleased with his advice. Use it carefully.

Tree of life	Revelation 22:14
Tree of life, river of life	Revelation 22:1-5
Vision of Christ, holding keys of death	Revelation 1:12-18
Wailing and anguish in streets	Amos 5:16, 17
Waiting on God	Psalm 130:5
Weary, comfort for	Isaiah 40:28-31
Wife and mother	Proverbs 31:10-31
Wisdom of God	Romans 11:33-36
Young man, godly	Proverbs 4:1-12
Youth and age	Ecclesiastes 12:1

Chapter Twelve

POEMS

Index of Topics

The following poems are alphabetical by title.

An Irish Airman Foresees His Death

I know that I shall meet my fate
Somewhere among the clouds above;
Those that I fight I do not hate,
Those that I guard I do not love;
My country is Kiltartan Cross,
My countrymen Kiltartan's poor,
No likely end could bring them loss
Or leave them happier than before.
Nor law, nor duty bade me fight,
Nor public men, nor cheering crowds,
A lonely impulse of delight
Drove to this tumult in the clouds;
I balanced all, brought all to mind,
The years to come seemed waste of breath,
A waste of breath the years behind
In balance with this life, this death.
               —William Butler Yeats

Character of a Happy Life

How happy is he born and taught
That serveth not another's will;
Whose armour is his honest thought,
And simple truth his utmost skill!

Whose passions not his masters are,
Whose soul is still prepared for death;
Untied unto the world by care
Of public fame, or private breath;

Who envies none that chance doth raise,
Nor vice; who never understood
How deepest wounds are given by praise;
Nor rules of state, but rules of good;

Who hath his life from rumors freed,
Whose conscience is his strong retreat;

Whose state can neither flatterers feed,
Nor ruin make oppressors great,

Who God doth late and early pray
More of His grace than gifts to lend;
And entertains the harmless day
With a religious book or friend;

This man is freed from servile bands
Of hope to rise, or fear to fall;
Lord of himself, though not of lands;
And having nothing, yet hath all.
　　　　　　　　—Sir Henry Wotton

Crossing the Bar

Sunset and evening star,
　　And one clear call for me!
And may there be no moaning of the bar,
　　When I put out to sea,

But such a tide as moving seems asleep,
　　Too full for sound and foam,
When that which drew from out the boundless deep
　　Turns again home.

Twilight and evening bell,
　　And after that the dark!
And may there be no sadness of farewell,
　　When I embark;

For tho' from out our bourne of Time and Place
　　The flood may bear me far,
I hope to see my Pilot face to face
　　When I have crossed the bar.
　　　　　　　—Alfred, Lord Tennyson

The Dead

These hearts were woven of human joys and cares,
　　Washed marvellously with sorrow, swift to mirth.
The years had given them kindness. Dawn was theirs,
　　And sunset, and the colors of the earth.

These had seen movement, and heard music; known
   Slumber and waking; loved; gone proudly friended;
Felt the quick stir of wonder; sat alone;
   Touched flowers and furs and cheeks. All this is ended.
There are waters blown by changing winds to laughter
   And lit by the rich skies, all day. And after,
Frost, with a gesture, stays the waves that dance
   And wandering loveliness. He leaves a white
Unbroken glory, a gathered radiance,
   A width, a shining peace, under the night.

—Rupert Brooke

Death

Death be not proud, though some have callèd thee
Mighty and dreadful, for, thou art not so;
For, those whom thou think'st thou dost overthrow
Die not, poor death; nor yet canst thou kill me.
From rest and sleep, which but thy pictures be,
Much pleasure; then from thee, much more must flow;
And soonest our best men with thee do go,
Rest of their bones, and soul's delivery.
Thou art slave to fate, chance, kings, and desperate men,
And dost with poison, war, and sickness dwell,
And poppy, or charms can make us sleep as well,
And better than thy stroke; Why swell'st thou then?
One short sleep past, we wake eternally,
And death shall be no more; death, thou shalt die.

—John Donne

The Death Bed

We watch'd her breathing thro' the night,
   Her breathing soft and low,
As in her breast the wave of life
   Kept heaving to and fro.

But when the morn came dim and sad
   And chill with early showers,
Her quiet eyelids closed — she had
   Another morn than ours.

—Thomas Hood

Dover Beach

The sea is calm tonight.
The tide is full; the moon lies fair
Upon the straits; on the French coast the light
Gleams and is gone; the cliffs of England stand
Glimmering and vast, out in the tranquil bay.

Come to the window, sweet is the night air!
Only, from the long line of spray
Where the sea meets the moon-blanched land,
Listen! you hear the grating roar
Of pebbles which the waves draw back, and fling,
At their return, up the high strand,
Begin, and cease, and then again begin,
With tremulous cadence slow, and bring
The eternal note of sadness in.

Sophocles long ago
Heard it on the Aegean, and it brought
Into his mind the turbid ebb and flow
Of human misery; we
Find also in the sound a thought,
Hearing it by this distant northern sea.

The Sea of Faith
Was once, too, at the full, and round earth's shore
Lay like the folds of a bright girdle furled.
But now I only hear
Its melancholy, long, withdrawing roar,
Retreating, to the breath
Of the night wind, down the vast edges drear
And naked shingles of the world.

Ah, love, let us be true
To one another! for the world, which seems
To lie before us like a land of dreams,
So various, so beautiful, so new,
Hath really neither joy, nor love, nor light,
Nor certitude, nor peace, nor help for pain;
And we are here as on a darkling plain

Swept with confused alarms of struggle and flight,
Where ignorant armies clash by night.

—Matthew Arnold

Finis

I strove with none, for none was worth my strife.
Nature I loved and, next to Nature, Art:
I warm'd both hands before the fire of life;
It sinks, and I am ready to depart.

—Walter Savage Landor

From the Heart . . .

When prayers are so many
   and feelings so high,
When Time is so hard and Pain so near,
   You look around and feel
   that a Christian is near.
The doorbell rings and a Christian is there,
   With pots and pans and food to share,
With soft-spoken words we need to hear . . .
   "We have so much love
   and food to share . . ."
A Christian we know is there.
A tear or two we shouldn't fear,
For God knows Heaven is near.

We thank God that we always
Have someone with love in their hearts
   and time to care!

—Charlie M. Bradshaw

Go from Me

Go from me. Yet I feel that I shall stand
Henceforward in thy shadow. Nevermore
Alone upon the threshold of my door
Of individual life, I shall command
The uses of my soul, nor lift my hand
Serenely in the sunshine as before,
Without the sense of that which I forbore, . . .

Thy touch upon the palm. The widest land
Doom takes to part us, leaves thy heart in mine
With pulses that beat double. What I do
And what I dream include thee, as the wine
Must taste of its own grapes. And when I sue
God for myself, he hears that name of thine,
And sees within my eyes the tears of two.

—Elizabeth Barrett Browning

The Harp That Once through Tara's Halls

The harp that once through Tara's halls
    The soul music shed,
Now hangs as mute on Tara's walls
    As if that soul were fled.
So sleeps the pride of former days,
    So glory's thrill is o'er,
And hearts that once beat high for praise
    Now feel that pulse no more!

No more to chiefs and ladies bright
    The harp of Tara swells;
The chord alone that breaks at night
    Its tale of ruin tells.
Thus Freedom now so seldom wakes,
    The only throb she gives
Is when some heart indignant breaks,
    To show that still she lives.

—Thomas Moore

Herrick's Cavalier

Give me that man that dares bestride
The active sea-horse, and with pride
Through that huge field of waters ride;
Who, with his looks too, can appease
The ruffling winds and raging seas
In midst of all their outrages.
This, this a virtuous man can do,
Sail against rocks, and split them too;
Ay, and a world of pikes pass through.

—Robert Herrick

High Flight

Oh! I have slipped the surly bonds of Earth,
And danced the skies on laughter-silvered wings;
Sunward I've climbed, and joined the tumbling mirth
Of sun-split clouds, and done a hundred things
You have not dreamed of — wheeled and soared and swung
High in the sunlit silence. Hov'ring there,
I've chased the shouting wind along, and flung
My eager craft through footless halls of air. . . .
Up, up the long, delirious, burning blue
I've topped the wind-swept heights with easy grace,
Where never lark or even eagle flew;
And while with silent, lifting mind I've trod
The high untrespassed sanctity of space,
Put out my hand and touched the face of God.

—John Magee

I Know That My Redeemer Lives

I know that my Redeemer lives,
     And ever prays for me;
A token of his love he gives,
     A pledge of liberty.

I find him lifting up my head;
     He brings salvation near;
His presence makes me free indeed,
     And he will soon appear.

He wills that I should holy be;
     What can withstand his will?
The counsel of his grace in me
     He surely shall fulfill.

When God is mine, and I am his,
     Of paradise possessed,
I taste unutterable bliss,
     And everlasting rest.

—Charles Wesley

The Journey Onwards

As slow our ship her foamy track
    Against the wind was cleaving,
Her trembling pennant still look'd back
    To that dear isle 'twas leaving.
So loth we part from all we love,
    From all the links that bind us;
So turn our hearts, as on we rove,
    To those we've left behind us!

When, round the bowl, of vanished years
    We talk with joyous seeming —
With smiles that might as well be tears,
    So faint, so sad their beaming;
While memory brings us back again
    Each early tie that twined us,
Oh, sweet's the cup that circles then
    To those we've left behind us!

And when in other climes we meet
    Some isle or vale enchanting,
Where all looks flowery, wild, and sweet,
    And nought but love is wanting;
We think how great had been our bliss
    If Heaven had but assign'd us
To live and die in scenes like this,
    With some we've left behind us!

As travelers oft look back at eve
    When eastward darkly going,
To gaze upon that light they leave
    Still faint behind them glowing,
So, when the close of pleasure's day
    To gloom hath near consign'd us,
We turn to catch one fading ray
    Of joy that's left behind us.

                    —Thomas Moore

Life! I Know Not What Thou Art

Life! I know not what thou art,
But know that thou and I must part;
And when, or how, or where we met
I own to me's a secret yet.
   Life! We've been long together
Through pleasant and through cloudy weather;
'Tis hard to part when friends are dear —
Perhaps 'twill cost a sigh, a tear;
— Then steal away, give little warning,
   Choose thine own time;
Say not Good Night, but in some brighter clime
   Bid me Good Morning.
              —Anna Letitia Barbauld

LXIII

O threats of Hell and Hopes of Paradise!
One thing at least is certain — *This* Life flies;
   One thing is certain and the rest Lies;
The Flower that once has blown for ever dies.
              —Edward Fitzgerald
        From the *Rubáiyát of Omar Khayyám*

LXIV

Strange, is it not? that of the myriads who
Before us pass'd the door of Darkness through,
   Not one returns to tell us of the Road,
Which to discover we must travel too.
              —Edward Fitzgerald
        From the *Rubáiyát of Omar Khayyám*

The Man Named Legion

The man named Legion asks for nothing more
Than his own rooftree, and the right to stand
Erect, unthreatened, on a square of land,
His children sturdy and his peace secure.
The world is wide, the generous earth could nourish
All men, and more, and still have room to spare.

So brief a while is his to breathe the air,
So cheap, so simple, all that he would cherish.

Out of such modest stuff his dreams are made,
But being humble, he is set at nought;
Harried, despoiled, most grievously betrayed.
And the pathetic little that he sought
Is held beyond his hope, beyond his touch —
That little, that impossible too much!

—Sara Henderson Hay

Monody

To have known him, to have loved him
    After loneness long;
And then to be estranged in life,
    And neither in the wrong;
And now for death to set his seal —
    Ease me, a little ease, my song!
By wintry hills his hermit-mound
    The sheeted snow-drifts drape,
And houseless there the snow-bird flits
    Beneath the fir-trees' crape:
Glazed now with ice the cloistral vine
    That hid the shyest grape.

—Herman Melville

O Captain! My Captain!

O Captain! my Captain! our fearful trip is done,
The ship has weather'd every rack, the prize we sought is won,
The port is near, the bells I hear, the people are exulting,
While follow eyes the steady keel, the vessel grim and daring;
    But O heart! heart! heart!
        O the bleeding drops of red,
            Where on the deck my Captain lies,
                Fallen cold and dead.

O Captain! my Captain! rise up and hear the bells;
Rise up — for you the flag is flung — for you the bugle trills,
For you bouquets and ribbon'd wreaths — for you the shores
    acrowding,

For you they call, the swaying mass, their eager faces turning;
Here Captain! dear father!
The arm beneath your head!
It is some dream that on the deck,
You've fallen cold and dead.

My Captain does not answer, his lips are pale and still,
My father does not feel my arm, he has no pulse nor will,
The ship is anchor'd safe and sound, its voyage closed and
done,
From fearful trip the victor ship comes in with object won:
Exult O shores, and ring O bells!
But I with mournful tread,
Walk the deck my Captain lies,
Fallen cold and dead.

—Walt Whitman

Oh, Yet We Trust

Oh yet we trust that somehow good
Will be the final goal of ill,
To pangs of nature, sins of will,
Defects of doubt, and taints of blood;

That nothing walks with aimless feet;
That not one life shall be destroyed,
Or cast as rubbish to the void,
When God hath made the pile complete;

That not a worm is cloven in vain;
That not a moth with vain desire
Is shrivelled in a fruitless fire,
Or but subserves another's gain.

Behold, we know not anything;
I can but trust that good shall fall
At last — far off — at last, to all,
And every winter change to spring.

So runs my dream: but what am I?
An infant crying in the night:
An infant crying for the light:
And with no language but a cry.

—Alfred Lord Tennyson

The Old Familiar Faces

I have had playmates, I have had companions
In my days of childhood, in my joyful school-days;
    All, all are gone, the old familiar faces.

I have been laughing, I have been carousing,
Drinking late, sitting late, with my bosom cronies;
    All, all are gone, the old familiar faces.

I loved a love once, fairest among women:
Closed are her doors on me, I must not see her —
    All, all are gone, the old familiar faces.

I have a friend, a kinder friend has no man:
Like an ingrate, I left my friend abruptly;
    Left him, to muse on the old familiar faces.

Ghost-like I paced round the haunts of my childhood,
Earth seem'd a desert I was bound to traverse,
    Seeking to find the old familiar faces.

Friend of my bosom, thou art more than a brother,
Why wert not thou born in my father's dwelling?
    So might we talk of the old familiar faces.

How some they have died, and some they have left me,
And some are taken from me; all are departed;
    All, all are gone, the old familiar faces.

—Charles Lamb

On an Infant Dying as Soon as Born

I saw where in the shroud did lurk
A curious frame of Nature's work;
A flow'ret crushed in the bud,
A nameless piece of Babyhood,
Was in her cradle-coffin lying;
Extinct, with scarce the sense of dying:
So soon to exchange the imprisoning womb
For darker closets of the tomb!
She did but ope an eye, and put
A clear beam forth, then straight up shut

For the long dark: ne'er more to see
Through glasses of mortality.
Riddle of destiny, who can show
What thy short visit meant, or know
What thy errand here below?
Shall we say, that Nature blind
Check'd her hand, and changed her mind,
Just when she had exactly wrought
A finish'd pattern without fault?
Could she flag, or could she tire,
Or lack'd she the Promethean fire
(With her nine moons' long workings sicken'd)
That should thy little limbs have quicken'd?
Limbs so firm, they seem'd to assure
Life of health, and days mature;
Woman's self in miniature!
Limbs so fair, they might supply
(Themselves now but cold imagery)
The sculptor to make Beauty by.
Or did the stern-eyed Fate descry
That babe or mother, one must die;
So in mercy left the stock
And cut the branch; to save the shock
Of young years widow'd, and the pain
When Single State comes back again
To the lone man who, 'reft of wife,
Thenceforward drags a maiméd life?
The economy of Heaven is dark,
And wisest clerks have miss'd the mark,
Why human buds, like this, should fall
More brief than fly ephemeral
That has his day; while shrivell'd crones
Stiffen with age to stocks and stones;
And crabbéd use the conscience sears
In sinners of an hundred years.
Mother's prattle, mother's kiss,
Baby fond, thou ne'er wilt miss:
Rites, which custom does impose,

Silver bells, and baby clothes;
Coral redder than those lips
Which pale death did late eclipse;
Music framed for infants' glee,
Whistle never tuned for thee;
Though thou want'st not, thou shalt have them,
Loving hearts were they which gave them.
Let not one be missing; nurse,
See them laid upon the hearse
Of infant slain by doom perverse.
Why should kings and nobles have
Pictured trophies to their grave,
And we, churls, to thee deny
Thy pretty toys with thee to lie —
A more harmless vanity?

—Charles Lamb

Prospice

Fear death? — to feel the fog in my throat,
    The mist in my face,
When the snows begin, and the blasts denote
    I am nearing the place,
The power of the night, the press of the storm,
    The post of the foe;
Where he stands, the Arch Fear in a visible form,
    Yet the strong man must go;
For the journey is done and the summit attained,
    And the barriers fall,
Though a battle's to fight ere the guerdon be gained,
    The reward for it all.
I was ever a fighter, so — one fight more,
    The best and the last!
I would hate that death bandaged my eyes, and forbore,
    And bade me creep past.
No! let me taste the whole of it, fare like my peers
    The heroes of old,
Bear the brunt, in a minute pay glad life's arrears
    Of pain, darkness and cold.

For sudden the worst turns the best to the brave,
　　The black minute's at end,
And the element's rage, the fiend-voices that rave,
　　Shall dwindle, shall blend,
Shall change, shall become first a peace out of pain,
　　Then a light, then thy breast,
O thou soul of my soul! I shall clasp thee again,
　　And with God be the rest!
　　　　　　　　　　　　—Robert Browning

Rabbi Ben Ezra

Grow old along with me!
The best is yet to be,
The last of life, for which the first was made:
Our times are in his hand
Who saith, "A whole I planned,
Youth shows but half; trust God: see all, nor be afraid!"
　　　　　　　　　　　　—Robert Browning

Requiescat

Strew on her roses, roses,
　　And never a spray of yew.
In quiet she reposes:
　　Ah! would that I did too.

Her mirth the world required:
　　She bathed it in smiles of glee.
But her heart was tired, tired,
　　And now they let her be.

Her life was turning, turning,
　　In mazes of heat and sound.
But for peace her soul was yearning,
　　And now peace laps her round.

Her cabin'd, ample Spirit,
　　It flutter'd and fail'd for breath.
To-night it doth inherit
　　The vasty hall of Death.
　　　　　　　　　　　　—Matthew Arnold

Revolutions

Like as the waves make towards the pebbled shore,
So do our minutes hasten to their end;
Each changing place with that which goes before,
In sequent toil all forwards do contend.
Nativity, once in the main of light,
Crawls to maturity, wherewith being crown'd,
Crooked eclipses 'gainst his glory fight,
And Time that gave doth now his gift confound.
Time doth transfix the flourish set on youth,
And delves the parallels in beauty's brow;
Feeds on the rarities of nature's truth,
And nothing stands but for his scythe to mow:
And yet, to times in hope, my verse shall stand
Praising thy worth, despite his cruel hand.

—William Shakespeare

The River of Life

The more we live, more brief appear
    Our life's succeeding stages:
A day to childhood seems a year,
    And years like passing ages.

The gladsome current of our youth,
    Ere passion yet disorders.
Steals lingering like a river smooth
    Along its grassy borders.

But as the careworn cheek grows wan,
    And sorrow's shafts fly thicker,
Ye stars, that measure life to man,
    Why seem your courses quicker?

When joys have lost their bloom and breath,
    And life itself is vapid,
Why, as we reach the Falls of death,
    Feel we its tide more rapid?

It may be strange — yet who would change
    Time's course to slower speeding,

When one by one our friends have gone
    And left our bosoms bleeding?

Heaven gives our years of fading strength
    Indemnifying fleetness;
And those of youth, a seeming length,
    Proportioned to their sweetness.
                —Thomas Campbell

Soldier Rest

Soldier, rest! thy warfare o'er,
    Sleep the sleep that knows not breaking;
Dream of battled fields no more,
    Days of danger, nights of waking.
In our isle's enchanted hall,
    Hands unseen thy couch are strewing,
Fairy strains of music fall,
    Every sense in slumber dewing.
Soldier, rest! thy warfare o'er,
Dream of fighting fields no more;
Sleep the sleep that knows not breaking,
Morn of toil, nor night of waking.

No rude sound shall reach thine ear,
    Armor's clang, or war-steed champing,
Trump nor pibroch summon here
    Mustering clan, or squadron tramping.
Yet the lark's shrill fife may come
    At the daybreak from the fallow,
And the bittern sound his drum,
    Booming from the sedgy shallow.
Ruder sounds shall none be near,
Guards nor warders challenge here;
Here's no war-steed's neigh and champing,
Shouting clans or squadrons stamping.

Huntsman, rest! thy chase is done,
    While your slumbrous spells assail ye,
Dream not, with the rising sun,
    Bugles here shall sound reveille.

Sleep! the deer is in his den;
    Sleep! thy hounds are by thee lying;
Sleep! nor dream in yonder glen
    How thy gallant steed lay dying.
Huntsman, rest! thy chase is done;
Think not of the rising sun,
For, at dawning to assail ye,
Here no bugles sound reveille.
    —Sir Walter Scott from *The Lady of the Lake*

Tempt Me No More

Tempt me no more; for I
Have known the lightning's hour,
The poet's inward pride,
The certainty of power.

Bayonets are closing round.
I shrink; yet must I wring
A living from despair
And out of steel a song.

Though song, though breath be short,
I'll share not the disgrace
Of those that ran away
Or never left the base.

Comrades, my tongue can speak
No comfortable words;
Calls to a forlorn hope
Give work and not rewards.

O keep the sickle sharp
And follow still the plow:
Others may reap, though some
See not the winter through.

Father who endest all,
Pity our broken sleep;
For we lie down with tears
And waken but to weep.

And if our blood alone
Will meet this iron earth,

Take it. It is well spent
Easing a savior's birth.

—C. Day Lewis

Thanatopsis

To him who in the love of Nature holds
Communion with her visible forms, she speaks
A various language; for his gayer hours
She has a voice of gladness, and a smile
And eloquence of beauty; and she glides
Into his darker musings, with a mild
And healing sympathy that steals away
Their sharpness ere he is aware. When thoughts
Of the last bitter hour come like a blight
Over thy spirit, and sad images
Of the stern agony, and shroud and pall
And breathless darkness and the narrow house
Make thee to shudder and grow sick at heart,
Go forth under the open sky and list
To Nature's teachings, while from all around —
Earth and her waters and the depths of air —
Comes a still voice:
Yet a few days, and thee
The all-beholding sun shall see no more
In all his course; nor yet in the cold ground,
Where thy pale form was laid with many tears,
Nor in the embrace of ocean, shall exist
Thy image. Earth, that nourished thee shall claim
Thy growth, to be resolved to earth again,
And, lost each human trace, surrendering up
Thine individual being, shalt thou go
To mix for ever with the elements,
To be a brother to the insensible rock
And to the sluggish clod, which the rude swain
Turns with his share, and treads upon; the oak
Shall send his roots abroad, and pierce thy mould.

Yet not to thine eternal resting-place
Shalt thou retire alone, nor couldst thou wish

Couch more magnificent. Thou shalt lie down
With patriarchs of the infant world, with kings,
The powerful of the earth, the wise, the good,
Fair forms, and hoary seers of ages past,
All in one mighty sepulchre. The hills
Rock-ribbed and ancient as the sun; the vales
Stretching in pensive quietness between;
The venerable woods, rivers that move
In majesty, and the complaining brooks
That make the meadows green; and, poured round all,
Old Ocean's gray and melancholy waste, —
Are but the solemn decorations all
Of the great tomb of man. The golden sun,
The planets, all the infinite host of heaven,
Are shining on the sad abodes of death,
Through the still lapse of ages. All that tread
The globe are but a handful to the tribes
That slumber in its bosom. Take the wings
Of morning, pierce the Barcan wilderness,
Or lose thyself in the contiguous woods
Where rolls the Oregon, and hears no sound
Save its own dashings; yet the dead are there,
And millions in those solitudes, since first
The flight of years began, have laid them down
In their last sleep: the dead reign there alone.
So shalt thou rest; and what if thou withdraw
In silence from the living, and no friend
Take note of thy departure? All that breathe
Will share thy destiny. The gay will laugh
When thou art gone, the solemn brood of care
Plod on, and each one as before will chase
His favorite phantom; yet all these shall leave
Their mirth and their employments, and shall come
And make their bed with thee. As the long train
Of ages glide away, the sons of men —
The youth in life's green spring, and he who goes
In the full strength of years, matron and maid,
The speechless babe, and the gray-headed man —

Shall one by one be gathered to thy side
By those who in their turn shall follow them.
So live that when thy summons come to join
The innumerable caravan which moves
To that mysterious realm where each shall take
His chamber in the silent halls of death,
Thou go not, like the quarry-slave at night,
Scourged to his dungeon, but, sustained and soothed
By an unfaltering trust, approach thy grave
Like one who wraps the drapery of his couch
About him and lies down to pleasant dreams.

—William Cullen Bryant

When I Have Fears That I May Cease to Be

When I have fears that I may cease to be
    Before my pen has gleaned from my teeming brain,
Before high piléd books, in charact'ry
    Hold like rich garners the full ripened grain;
When I behold, upon the night's starred face,
    Huge cloudy symbols of a high romance,
And think that I may never live to trace
    Their shadows, with the magic hand of chance;
And when I feel, fair creature of an hour,
    That I shall never look upon thee more,
Never have relish in the faery power
    Of unreflecting love; — then on the shore
Of the wide world I stand alone, and think
    Till love and fame to nothingness do sink.

—John Keats

Youth and Age

Verse, a breeze 'mid blossoms straying,
    Where Hope clung feeding, like a bee —
Both were mine! Life went a-maying
    With Nature, Hope, and Poesy,
        When I was young.

When I was young? Ah, woeful When.
Ah, for the change 'twixt Now and Then!

This breathing house not built with hands,
    This body that does me grievous wrong,
O'er aery cliffs and glittering sands
    How lightly then it flash'd along:
Like those trim skiffs, unknown of yore,
    On winding lakes and rivers wide,
That ask no aid of sail or oar,
    That fear no spite of wind or tide!
Nought cared this body for wind or weather
When Youth and I lived in't together.

Flowers are lovely; Love is flower-like;
    Friendship is a sheltering tree;
O! the joys, that came down shower-like,
    Of friendship, Love, and Liberty,
        Ere I was old!

Ere I was old? Ah, woeful Ere,
Which tells me, Youth's no longer here!
O Youth! for years so many and sweet
    'Tis known that Thou and I were one,
I'll think it but a fond conceit —
    It cannot be that thou art gone!
Thy vesper bell hath not yet toll'd:
And thou wert ay a masker bold!
What strange disguise hast now put on
To make believe that thou art gone?
I see these locks in silvery slips,
    This drooping gait, this alter'd size:
But Springtide blossoms on thy lips,
    And tears take sunshine from thine eyes!
Life is but thought: so think I will
That Youth and I are housemates still.

Dew-drops are the gems of morning,
    But the tear of mournful eve!
Where no hope is, life's a warning
    That only serves to make us grieve
        When we are old:

That only serves to make us grieve
With oft and tedious taking-leave,

Like some poor nigh-related guest
That may not rudely be dismist,
Yet hath outstay'd of his welcome while,
And tells the jest without the smile.
                    —Samuel Taylor Coleridge

The following selections are from *Found*, by Pearl Pierson

Though darkness ever grows more dense
We know that Light will come, and hence
This gathering darkness but portends
That coming Day when darkness ends!
We look upon the earth, and sigh —
We lift our eyes: Hope tints the sky
With dawning Light; and each bright ray
Brings richer promise of the Day —
        God Is — God Is — GOD IS!

A widow, grieving for her son,
An act of tender mercy done,
'Twas thus the Master's race was run.
Man's trust in God was thus begun:
And thus man's faith today is won.

A kindly word of sympathy,
A whisper of eternity —
'Tis thus our soul is made to see
That Christ has power to set us free —
'Tis thus, dear Lord, we come to Thee.

He does not fear the raging sea,
As on the breast of Galilee,
Serene and calm, and Spirit free,
        Our Saviour sleeps.

Ah, why should any mortal fear
The winds of life? the Lord is near;
He speaks in accents calm and clear:
        Believe in me.

We find new hope when we confess
Dependence on His righteousness:
In times of storm, or deep distress,
    He giveth peace.

In cycle growth, life moves along:
    The seed, the leaf, the plant, the bloom —
Then seed again, which does not grow
Until it rises from the tomb
In which it leaves its outer shell.
    The kernel, where life must begin,
Grows warm with hope of coming spring —
    And life revives, where life has been.

We live, (or think we live), until
    We realize that we must die:
We must forsake these earthly shells,
    E'er Living Water can supply
Eternal life to souls within
    These outer shells of earthy clay —
Yes, we must die to things of earth
    To find our resurrection day.

Forever the accepted time
Is now! The onward, upward climb
Grows brighter every step we take —
As happier, more wide awake
We hasten to behold the face
Of Him who saves us by His grace.
With grace He doth our hearts endow
To live in the eternal now.

Eternity is very real,
When through the Spirit we can feel
The wounded hand of Him who gave
His life to lift us from the grave:
And oh, how glorious grows the way
When we have learned to live today!
Yes, Jesus came to teach us how
To live in the eternal now.

O Loving Father, give us seeing eyes!
We view the glory of Thy arching skies,
And know that in Thy house no darkness is —
For Christ is Light; and all Thy mansions His.
We do not live until we see His light
And glory in the greatness of His might!

When we suffer grief and anguish,
    To our hearts, now wracked with pain,
Comes the oft repeated question,
    Did the Master die in vain?

No! He died to save the spirits
    Living in the haunts of death —
Jesus is the resurrection!
    There is healing in His breath!

Life is found amidst destruction —
    Gold is found amidst alloy —
Thus our path of pain and sorrow
    Leads, through Christ, to heights of joy.

And the joys of Christian living
    Are not ended by the tomb:
Jesus leads us through the darkness
    To a path where roses bloom.

Some day the Master Shepherd
    Will come to claim His own;
And there will be rejoicing
    Where ever He is known:
How blest will be that shepherd
    Whose sheep have found the way
Into that larger Sheepfold
    From which they will not stray!

O precious Shepherd of our souls,
Thy love each wandering lamb consoles.
All we like sheep have gone astray,
    And God hath laid our sins on Thee —

Yet Thou hast glorified His name
     And set our ransomed spirits free.
Thy love hath silenced fear and doubt —
Thou hast encompassed us about
With arms of love. In Thee is found
     The peace of Thy forgiving grace.
And through Thy glorious victory
     We now behold Thee, face to face!

Chapter Thirteen

HYMNS

Listed in this section are the titles of 110 hymns, many of which have been used at funeral and memorial services I've conducted. Others have lyrics I think are suitable. These can be found in contemporary hymnals. Of course, the list is not exhaustive.

Families are often so dazed and numb that it is hard for them to recollect and think. Remembering the titles of hymns the deceased would have liked or chosen may be difficult. You can be of assistance by providing the titles of several hymns from which they can choose. Make sure, however, that the musicians performing at the service know the songs and/or have the music available.

I always suggest that the sadder songs be used in the first part of the service and the more hopeful, upbeat songs be used at the close to affirm the resurrection.

Occasionally, families will request classical music, such as Beethoven and Mozart. You may also have families request popular songs. You will have to decide the appropriateness based on content of the words.

Abide with Me
Abide with Me; 'tis Eventide
Above the Bright Blue
Amazing Grace
An Empty Mansion
As the Life of a Flower
Asleep in Jesus
At Evening Time

Be Not Dismayed
Be with Me, Lord
Beautiful Isle of Somewhere
Beautiful Valley of Eden
Because He Lives
Beyond the Sunset
Beyond this Land of Parting
Blessed Assurance
Brief Life Is Here Our Portion

Come, Ye Disconsolate

Does Jesus Care?

Every Cloud Has a Silver Lining
Eternal Father, Strong to Save

Face to Face
Farther Along
For All the Saints

God Shall Wipe Away
God Will Take Care of You
God's Tomorrow
Going Home

Haven of Rest
Heaven
Heaven Holds All to Me
Heaven Will Surely Be
Home of the Soul
How Beautiful Heaven Must Be

How Great Thou Art

I Have Heard of a Land
I Know Not Why God's
    Wondrous Grace
I'll Fly Away
I'll Meet You in the Morning
I'm a Pilgrim
If We Never Meet Again
Immortal Love, Forever Full
In Heavenly Love Abiding
In the Garden
In the Land of Fadeless Day
In the Shadow of His Wings
It Is Well With My Soul

Jesus, Rose of Sharon
Jesus Knows and Cares
Just a Rose Will Do

Lead, Kindly Light

My God and I
My Soul in Sad Exile

Near to the Heart of God
Nearer, My God, to Thee
Nearer, Still Nearer
Never Grow Old
No Tears in Heaven
Nobody Knows But Jesus
Not Now But in the Coming
    Years

O Heart, Bowed Down with
    Sorrow
O Love that Wilt Not Let Me Go
Oh, They Tell Me of a Home
Oh, Think of the Home Over
    There
One Sweetly Solemn Thought

Only in Thee

Peace, Perfect Peace
Precious Lord, Take My Hand
Precious Memories
Prepare to Meet Thy God

Rock of Ages

Safe in the Arms of Jesus
Safe in the Harbor
Saved by Grace
Shall We Gather at the River?
Shall We Meet Beyond?
Someday the Silver Cord Will
    Break
Sometime, We'll Understand
Sunset and Evening Star
Sweet Peace, the Gift of God's
    Love

Tarry with Me
That Heavenly Home
The Last Mile of the Way
The Old Rugged Cross
The Sands Have Been Washed
The Sands of Time
The Touch of His Hand on Mine
The Way of the Cross

There Are Loved Ones
There Will Be Light
There's a Land Beyond the River
There's a Land that Is Fairer
    (Sweet By and By)
This World Is Not My Home
Thou My Everlasting Portion
To Canaan's Land I'm on My
    Way

Under His Wings
Unto the Hills

Victory in Jesus

We Are Going Down
We Shall Meet Someday
What a Friend We Have in Jesus
When All My Labors and Trials
When Comes to the Weary a
    Blessed Release
When Day's Shadows
When I Shall Come
When the Roll Is Called Up
    Yonder
Where the Roses Never Fade
Will the Circle Be Unbroken?

Yes, for Me

Chapter Fourteen

COMMITTAL SERVICES

EXAMPLE OF A COMMITTAL PRAYER

Dear Heavenly Father:

It is difficult for us to say goodbye to _____. We now commit him/her to your care, knowing and acknowledging that you are the God of all the universe, that you have created us and redeemed us in Christ, and that you are always a God of love and compassion.

We pray that you will console and comfort this family (use names where appropriate). Help them in their pain, tears, and loss to see you and your love and to understand you more completely. Please surround them with your warm, loving arms of compassion.

We know that you will call us all before you on that great, final day. Help us to find our confidence in our Lord and Savior, Jesus Christ, who died for us, who won complete victory over death for us, and who taught us to say: (recite here the Lord's Prayer if you so desire, and close in Jesus' name).

COMMITTAL SERVICE POETRY

The following poems were written by my aunt Pearl Pierson when her son was accidentally killed. I believe any of them would be appropriate to read at a committal service.

Reason for Our Hope

Those loving eyes are closed in sleep;
Yet we have hope, and do not weep
For him who goes to dwell above
Where all is joy, and peace and love.

That tongue, whose gentle kindly word
The eager little children heard,
Is quiet now; yet we rejoice
In hope again to hear that voice.

Those active hands no longer toil
Amid the rocky earthly soil:
We view the fruitage of their work,
And thank the Lord they did not shirk.

Those ready feet, so quick to run
On errands here for everyone
Are now at rest, no more to roam.
A living soul has journeyed home.

We look above with hope secure
In him whose Word is true and sure,
Eternal, endless in its scope.
We look to Christ in blessed hope.

1 Peter 3:15-22

God's Eternal Love

We sorrow not as they who have no hope,
For God has given us a vision of the scope
    Of his eternal love.
What blessed hope is ours, who pray and wait
To gain an entrance to yon pearly gate!
For all our losses God will compensate.
    He lives! He reigns above!

When God so loved the world he gave
His Son to lift us from the grave,
    Should we repine and weep?
We look to God in praise, and say,

"Thy will be done." We hope and pray
For added strength from day to day
    God's holy Word to keep.

                   John 3:16

We Find It So

So much we do not understand—
    So much we do not know—
We trust all things with Thee, dear Lord,
    And it is better so.
Thy way will make our faith secure;
Thy way will make our hope endure;
Thy way will make our blessings sure.
    Thy way is best; we find it so.

O Father God, Thy way is best,
    And we have found it so.
We find in Thee our peace and rest;
    In Thee we live and grow.
Thy way will make us good and wise,
For in Thy way of life we rise
To dwell with Thee beyond the skies.
    Thy way is best; we find it so.

                 Psalm 1:1-3

His Way Is Best

His way is best, we find it so.
There is so much we do not know.
We trust in God and find sweet rest:
Whatever comes, his way is best.

His way is best. We do not grieve
When sorrow comes, for we believe
That righteous souls awaken blest.
We have bright hope. God's way is best.

His way is best. He conquered death.
He gives our souls eternal breath.
He gives us strength to meet each test.
We trust in God. His way is best.

His way is best. It always is.
He cares for us for we are his.
He comforts all who have confessed
Their trust in him. His way is best.

Proverbs 3:5-6; 4:18

A Great Experience

A great experience awaits
The living soul at heaven's gates,
Yet still with trembling heart we fear
The hand of death as it draws near.

The great experience of death
But robs our frame of mortal breath,
And gives our soul a full release
To rise to joyous lands of peace.

The great experience of life,
Beyond all sorrow, pain, and strife,
Is worth our toil and struggle here,
And all that mortal man holds dear.

A great experience above
Awaits for all who know the love
Of him who rules the earth and sky,
And calls us home to dwell on high.

Philippians 1:21

Remember, O Father, that I am of clay;
Thou gavest me life, thou canst take it away.
In Jesus I glory, for I am so weak.
Oh, give me the wisdom I earnestly seek.
All honor and power and glory are thine;
Oh, grant me a portion of riches divine.
Thy grace fills my soul with thine infinite love,
Yet still I am seeking more light from above.
I praise thee for blessings again and again.
May thine be the glory forever. Amen.

In Thy Hand

I did not know which way to go
   to reach the Promised Land.
I heard One say, "I am the way";
   then Jesus took my hand.

My light was dim, I turned to him;
   he helped me understand.
The Master came and spoke my name;
   he took my trembling hand.

O God above, how sweet thy love!
   I seek thy blest command.
Thy will for me, oh let it be
   forever in thy hand.

Until the end, O Savior Friend,
   all things are in thy hand.
Thy love divine has made me thine,
   I trust thy guiding hand.

John 14:1-21

O Death, Where Is Thy Victory

O death, where is thy victory?
   O death, where is thy sting?
Thanks be to God for victory!
   In Jesus Christ we sing
Of life, sweet life, abundant life,
   Of life beyond the grave.
We have eternal life in Christ,
   The life he freely gave.

O grave, where is thy victory?
   O death, where is thy power?
Thanks be to God for victory,
   For strength to meet each hour!
In Christ we find the way of life—
   The joyous glory-way
To shining mansions in the skies
   Where we may dwell someday.

For death there is no victory!
   The sting of earthly sin
Is swallowed up in victory!
   Through Christ we enter in
The glories of eternal life.
   Though still on earth we trod,
We know that we have found the way
   To endless life with God.
               1 Corinthians 15:50-57

Selected Reading List

Comfort Those Who Mourn: How to Preach Personalized Funeral Messages by Kenn Filkins, College Press Publishing Company, Joplin, MO, 1992.

Comforting the Bereaved by W. and D. Wiersbe, Moody Press, Chicago, 1985.

Comforting Those Who Grieve by D. Manning, Harper & Row, San Francisco, 1985.

Death: Confronting the Reality by W. Phipps, John Knox, Atlanta, 1987.

Death: The Final Stage of Growth by Elisabeth Kübler-Ross, Prentice-Hall, Englewood Cliffs, NJ, 1975.

Difficult Funeral Services by James L. Christensen, Fleming H. Revell Company, Old Tappan, NJ, 1985.

Leadership Handbooks of Practical Theology, Volume One, Word & Worship, General Editor, James D. Berkley, Baker Book House, Grand Rapids, MI, 1992, pp. 461–499.

Mortal Matters by S. Engram, Andrews & McMeel, Kansas City, MO, 1990.

On Death and Dying: What the Dying Have to Teach Doctors, Nurses, Clergy and Their Own Families by Elisabeth Kübler-Ross, Macmillan Publishing Co., New York, 1970.

The
Wedding
HANDBOOK

The Wedding Handbook

Introduction

"I would rather do five funerals than do one wedding," said my minister friend, Gregg Johnson. Is he possessed of some strange fixation? No. In fact he appears well balanced. "In funerals we deal with one or two emotions," he says. "In weddings we encounter scores of them." As you probably know, not just the emotions of ecstasy, ardor, and elation surround wedding altars. At times, white dinner jackets and formal gowns little conceal festering ire and untiring envy. If we attempt to officiate without knowing of the potential for conflict, we might begin favoring funerals over weddings fifty to one.

Measured by the number of marriages performed, my experience likely doesn't compare to most clergy who have spent an equal time in ministry. Others can claim more occasions of officiating at weddings, especially very formal ones. So what qualifies me to write on the subject of weddings?

A doctor friend once related to me the advantages of doing internships and residencies at the Los Angeles County-University of Southern California Medical Center. Those who trained there got to treat persons with almost every conceivable disease, injury, and congenital problem. I never expected, when my wife and I moved to Los Angeles four decades ago, that we would experience exposure to people of such diverse backgrounds.

My tenure in Hollywood introduced me to a ten-lifetime share of different people. These included the unprincipled, amoral, and immoral. One evening I performed a marriage service for two actors. He played a major role in a made-for-television movie, and she a minor part. During the time of counseling they attended worship services and seemed interested in the Lord. We held the ceremony in the Hollywood American Legion Hall, where scores of guests enjoyed a full-course dinner.

Several well-known stars attended, and quite possibly many unknowns at the time who have later attained stardom. The groom has since made numerous movies. At the reception that night, my wife noticed that the women seated at our table went to the rest room in shifts of two. As each duo returned they handed a small black purse to the next two. Our dinner companions never invited Norma on those trips or to take the purse. We're thankful. In retrospect we agreed that the purse likely contained cocaine.

During my twenty-eight years in Hollywood, I performed wedding ceremonies at the top of Mount Hollywood, on rooftops, and at the Beverly Hills Hotel with swans swimming nearby. I conducted them in the mountains near Santa Barbara and across the continent in Baltimore. I helped couples with their vows in dingy apartment buildings under the scrutiny of vermin, and experienced the joy of hearing vows spoken in the accents of scores of languages. Ages of the couples involved ranged from seventeen to eighty.

Services included those for couples of numerous cultures and frequently for cross-cultural partners. I had to overlook the mother of one bride who ran up to the front to adjust her daughter's dress. In their particular Asian country, it was customary. Possibly other things I shouldn't have overlooked.

One of our personal challenges was to not disintegrate as we plunged into that blending pail known as Southern California. The diversity of the people gave occasions of delight as well as challenge. At a wedding of a couple from two different Asian cultures, an Italian opera singer was asked to sing a solo. He walked up, stood near a front pew, and sang so loudly that we feared two things: The groom's family's doom to salivary inundation, and second, the integrity of the building's back wall.

Norma and I also experienced rewards we shall treasure always. One of those is the joy of being part of a diverse extended family. Somewhere out there is a very bald Chinese son who "adopted" us after I performed a ceremony for him and his lovely wife many years ago. Not long before my retirement, I officiated at the service of a Mexican-American who met and fell in love with one of the members of our church. She is an Armenian woman who was born in Cairo, Egypt.

What began occurring several decades ago in multicultural cities such as Los Angeles now takes place all over the U.S. In 1990, sixty-five percent of Japanese-Americans married outside their race. Currently seventy percent of Native Americans marry outside theirs. Ministers must be prepared with biblical help for people whose cultures, colors, races, or religions will be blended in matrimony. In chapter five, you will find some suggestions on dealing with mixed marriages.

BIBLICAL PRECEDENTS FOR MARRIAGE CEREMONIES

We don't know how much of a ceremony the Lord provided Adam and Eve when he first gave Adam's rib to Eve, and Eve's hand to Adam in marriage. Angels probably witnessed it with curiosity. But the first couple had no peers to give approval or voice objection.

Much later in biblical history, after Sarah's death, Abraham's chief servant brought Rebekah from Haran to the Negev as a bride for Isaac. "Isaac brought her into the tent of his mother Sarah, and he married Rebekah," the Genesis account tersely records. "So she became his wife, and he loved her" (Genesis 24:66, 67). Was some ritual performed to affirm that union? No evidence for it exists.

But the Old Testament reveals some firmly fixed customs. Although young men probably found opportunities to meet young ladies at the local watering holes (I use that term literally — apparently it fell to young women in Bible times to obtain water from the wells), the father of the groom probably arranged the marriage with the bride's father. The fathers also negotiated agreement on a price for the bride, the dowry. Abraham's servant evidently carried the equivalent of Rodeo Drive jewelry and an unlimited checking account in order to get a satisfactory bride for the grieving Isaac. The proffered nose ring hooked Rebekah.

Saul attempted to entrap David by setting a seemingly impossible and gruesome dowry for Michal, his daughter. He demanded a hundred Philistine foreskins. David circumvented Saul's ploy; he brought twice that amount (1 Samuel 18:27). The ardent Shechem offered to pay any price to obtain Dinah, daughter of Jacob (Genesis 34:12). He paid a higher rate than he could have imagined. Some Shechemite should have urged him to circumspection.

The Philistines evidently conducted long, costly ceremonies. Samson was to have thirty attendants when marrying the young woman from Timnah. The event lasted seven days (Judges 14).

Jesus attended weddings, and he used wedding customs familiar to his contemporaries to illustrate lessons about the Kingdom of God. One of the most compelling of these is the Parable of the Ten Virgins. In Jesus' day the host supplied all the wedding guests with clothes for the occasion upon their arrival at the ceremony. That practice explains the puzzling parable found in Matthew 22:1-14. Why did the wedding guest who didn't wear his robe receive such harsh treatment? The question about the absence of his garment left him speechless. He had no excuse. Too inconsiderate and lazy to clean up and change at the door, he got ejected by the king's bouncers.

No evidence exists that Jesus performed any marriage ceremonies. To my knowledge, neither did any elder or evangelist mentioned in the New Testament. Present-day ministers probably owe their involvement to the precedents of priests and rabbis.

Now we see evolving customs and traditions affected by ethnicity, religion, local, and family customs. Television, movies, and magazines likely shape views, traditions, and customs as much as any other factor in the late twentieth century.

As every minister soon learns, launching people into the uncertain space of marriage can be a scary process. It's frightening not just for the young couples out there in those fragile capsules sometimes inaccurately or prematurely labeled "wedded bliss." The launch can panic ministers right out of their clerical robes.

THE SPECIAL CHALLENGES OF CONDUCTING MARRIAGE SERVICES

Funerals confront us with intense guilt and fear. But heightened, impassioned cries echo around wedding settings, too. The potential for ugly emotions resides in almost every wedding context. Be ready to administer massive doses of love.

Consider the question, What's necessary to perform a marriage service? We face bewildering arrays of questions that lack ready answers. Are we qualified legally and by our church to unite people in marriage? Do the candidates need blood tests and birth certificates? What do we do when there are previous marriages? How do we deal with the increasing incidence of cohabitation? What if they want to say their own vows or if they come from different cultures? How many witnesses are necessary? What should we do if the couple wants to get married in a hot air balloon, underwater, or at the beach? What if the bride and her mother disagree on arrangements, especially if the bride's parents are paying for the wedding? What do we say when parents disapprove of the prospective mate?

I was a novice when I performed my first wedding ceremony, far too inexperienced to help guide a couple into the future. In fact I was almost totally ignorant of wedding customs. I had attended a half dozen services at the most. That number included my own; Norma and I had been married less than a year.

To prepare myself to perform the wedding, I purchased a minister's manual, which furnished some orders of services. I also sought the advice of an older minister. I doubt whether I gave the couple any counseling. They made their request to me through a mutual friend.

We held the ceremony in a private residence. In my haste and ignorance, I spent little time looking in my manual for guidance about where to have the parties stand. I thought my manual illustrated a diagram with the groom to my left and the bride on my right. But I vividly recalled that when Norma and I got married, I stood on the minister's right. The minister had years of experience so must have been correct, I reasoned. That's the way I lined up those first candidates.

Then I looked at my manual again. Nervously I noted that I had lined up the bridal party opposite of what the diagram showed. So before I started the ceremony, I changed the people around to conform to the instructions in my manual. Off-handedly I stated that for some reason at my wedding we had lined up differently. The groom good-naturedly asked me, "Are you sure yours was legal?"

Why were Norma and I lined up on the "wrong side" of the minister? We weren't really. I just realized this today as I write that my view of it all these years has been backward. How so? I was a participant, not the minister. Also the bridal party faced the audience. Be sure to get it straight before you arrive at your first rehearsal. In case you are wondering, ours was legal.

I wish I could say that that first nuptial service was the only wedding trial I experienced. You will do well if you err only once. One reason I wrote this manual was to help others avoid some of the mistakes I made early in my ministry.

One of my most frustrating experiences resulted from my early concern about offending people. I now know that was simply fear and trembling in the presence of people who appeared more successful than I. We need to work through this to succeed in all phases of ministry and of life.

This next experience occurred after I finished my schooling and first preached for the Church of Christ in Hollywood. The son of an influential and wealthy couple in the area asked me to perform his marriage service. Both of his parents intimidated me. Their son met and wanted to marry a very nice young lady who came from a modest background. The groom's parents expressed open disdain — and not just for the bride's parents. They despised the bride, too. Few people met their standards. Later I learned they even hated each other. All that hate should have signaled to me to bow out. I sincerely thought, though, that with a little help and counseling the young couple might make it. It's even possible they could have had they moved two thousand miles from both sets of parents.

The couple showed promise in the marriage counseling sessions. We even got through the rehearsal without difficulty. But disaster struck early on the afternoon of the wedding. A local florist delivered extra sets of floral arrangements and corsages.

The groom's parents assumed that the less-well-off bride's parents wouldn't, or perhaps couldn't, provide adequate bouquets, corsages, etc. They duplicated every floral piece. That's not all. They ordered far more elaborate arrangements than the originals. They even arranged for a floral archway and had it placed where the bride and groom were to stand. I didn't know it was there until I walked in with the groom and groomsmen as the music began for the procession. It crowded everyone. It obscured my vision. None of the attendants knew where to stand.

Earlier the bride's father had become incensed over some matter. He came into the assembly room for the groomsmen and argued furiously with the groom's father. They shouted at each other so loudly that we asked those in charge of the music to increase the volume in order to dampen the din. We finally got them separated so we could begin our ceremony of love.

Of all the honoraria I received, I probably recall the one from that wedding the most vividly. The best man paid me as is customary, but the groom probably didn't know what I received. The best man was the high rolling, big spending father of the groom. After the ceremony was over, he pulled a huge wad of cash out of his pocket, peeled off two one-dollar bills, and proudly gave them to me as if they were thousands.

At the reception, the bride's father, smarting from numerous offenses, bewailed his predicament. As I sat next to him he gave notice, "I'm going to give him (the groom) one year. If he doesn't treat her right, I'm taking her back." At least I had the presence of mind to remind him what it meant when he gave his daughter away. By that time, however, my pride hurt too, because of that miserly fee tendered by the groom's father.

I wish I could say that I've learned all my lessons well. Although that two dollar wedding sticks in my mind as if superglued, Norma likes to talk about the time I invested much time, planning, and energy helping another couple from the Hollywood community. We spent many hours in counseling, rehearsals, and a fairly elaborate wedding. From that one I took home a loaf of monkey bread.

Norma and I made an agreement years ago whereby she got all monies received for weddings I performed, and I kept honoraria from funerals. I am not intimating that my chief motivation in performing marriage ceremonies was the stipend for my wife. In fact I gladly, with her approval, did many marriage services gratis. But laborers are always worthy of their hire.

Clear understanding of expectations is always necessary. Express candidly what you expect. Couples also need to understand their obligations. Why this is so important, and how we can communicate this effectively will be covered in chapter three.

SETTING GOALS FOR MARRIAGES AND YOUR PRIORITIES

We Christian ministers need to take wedding participants past the starry-eyed images portrayed and impressed on Celluloid and lithograph. We want to use these opportunities to help people discover and use principles for finding joy in this relationship to which the Lord gave primary status in Scripture.

Our counsel and the principles we recommend may make the difference between a marriage that gives lasting glory to God and one that becomes another digit in divorce statistics. An enduring marriage based on the teachings of Jesus results in a happier couple. It also creates contented offspring and more stable societies.

As you may have recognized or experienced, performing wedding ceremonies is extremely time consuming. In urban and rural areas, satisfied couples often make referrals. Look at the cost-effectiveness of these opportunities in terms of the main focus of your ministry. If you emphasize evangelism, you will probably want to weigh carefully the time required to counsel and rehearse for wedding ceremonies. In chapter three, I will suggest ways to set fees and to make choices about the types of services you perform.

You can accomplish several important goals with an informed, proper approach to the work of officiating. This assumes you want to honor God by making the proclamation of the good news about Jesus your first priority. In later years I attempted to make that my number one goal.

When non-Christian couples request that I perform marriage ceremonies for them, I usually insist that they complete a Bible study with me. It's designed to bring lives into submission to Jesus. The study helps me to identify areas of strength and weakness that each one brings to the marriage. It's extremely difficult to help those unwilling to yield themselves to the Lord and his principles.

On the other hand, officiating at wedding ceremonies provides ministers with good opportunities to acquaint people with the good news. Many couples gain an experience of the joy and satisfaction in knowing and being known by Jesus.

Chapter One

GOAL SETTING

Before we can decide how to perform marriage services, we need to clarify some goals and objectives. First, what goals should married couples set out to accomplish? Second, what objectives do we have for the service itself?

Our first stated goal, "What newly married couples should set out to accomplish," may seem beyond the scope of this book. Every married couple has different goals, and often the partners themselves have conflicting objectives. But I believe we should call all people to certain purposes in life. The primary one is to honor God with our lives and our marriages.

HONORING GOD

How does the Lord want us to honor him? In the Genesis account, immediately after He created Eve, the Lord established the one-flesh relationship of husband and wife. What does the one-flesh concept intimate? An analogy from our bodies helps.

A few persons have related to me circumstances of severe infections in the flesh of their legs. The disease seemed life threatening. Doctors advised amputation. Those afflicted risked extreme pain, even death in order to preserve those limbs. It was their flesh. They didn't want to part with it regardless of medical advice.

149

Scripture teaches us that the new "flesh" which we gain in marriage we should consider equally as dear as our own flesh. "No one ever hated his own body, but he feeds and cares for it," said Paul (Ephesians 5:29). This is one form of masochism we can all treat.

Jesus spoke of the granite-like hearts among the citizens of ancient Israel. That condition eventually caused an easing of the laws concerning divorce. But the Lord intended the one-flesh concept be observed, Jesus explained, because that's what our creator has always desired for us (see Matthew 19:1-13).

As the prophet, Malachi, warned, those who disregarded the sanctity of one-flesh had neglected the Lord's counsel. In Malachi's day, intense, lachrymal ritual gained not one drop of mercy from God. Why didn't the Lord look kindly on Israel's temple-drenching weeping and wailing? As the prophet explained (2:14), "It is because the LORD is acting as the witness between you and the wife of your youth, because you have broken faith with her, though she is your partner, the wife of your marriage covenant." The Lord witnesses our lifetime marriage covenants, and he is not the sort the Mafia can send into hiding.

Paul elaborated on the love required for that one-flesh relationship in Ephesians chapter 5. We should be familiar with it so we can review it carefully and thoughtfully with candidates. Each partner in the marriage should understand and be willing to carry out his/her responsibilities. Couples unaware of the principles of Ephesians 5 should probably not be let out for recess.

The marriage relationship symbolizes God's love for his people. In Isaiah 61:10, the servant told how he was "clothed . . . with garments of salvation and arrayed . . . in a robe of righteousness, as a bridegroom adorns his head like a priest, and as a bride adorns herself . . . ." The Lord reassured faithless Israel in Hosea 2:19, 20, that in the future she will be "betrothed to him forever in righteousness, justice, love and compassion. And you will acknowledge the LORD" (paraphrase). The Lord takes our marriage relationships seriously. He expects us to do the same. He insists that both parties bring and maintain the pure, self-giving love of Jesus. Too many couples are self-loving and unsure.

Jesus clearly heads his Church. The New Testament calls husbands/fathers to oversee their families as well. How is this done?

ROLES OF FATHERS WITHIN CHANGING TRADITIONS

The traditional roles of husband and wife are in fitful transition. Anguished change is occurring in the U.S. and all over the world. I use the term "traditional" advisedly because those roles have been evolving and in flux for centuries. Ethnic, special interest, and media influences all call for a reprogramming of marital roles. We fix our VCRs with far more facility.

We discover a curiosity when we read the role of the worthy woman-wife described by King Lemuel in Proverbs 31. If we hope for a wealth of support there for the "traditional" wife and husband duties, we'll come back destitute. We find little help in the rest of the Old Testament. Paul outlined mutual sexual obligations in 1 Corinthians 7. He described the loving approaches needed by husband and wife in Ephesians 5-6. In 1 Peter, that apostle gave advice to wives. Other than in these passages, specifics appear rarely in the New Testament. We should probably call the stereotypical roles "contemporary-traditional." The term "biblical" may not apply.

List all the duties the worthy woman performed as described in Proverbs 31. It leaves you with a ledger that has awkward imbalances. Her husband had it easy. He merely sat with other equally fortunate men at a prominent place near the city gate looking wise and proud.

One of the greatest sources of stress in present day marriages arises from the inability of couples to define their separate roles. Norma and I have altered our household responsibilities over the past few years. When we first married, I usually maintained the car (we could barely afford one then). But many times she worked alongside me under old Chevrolets helping me replace u-joints and transmissions. I did most of the yard work. Well, a good portion.

She performed the majority of in-house chores. Her tasks were far more demanding and regular. She prepared meals, mostly with inadequate funds that I provided, did the dishes, the laundry, and the ironing. She kept the children clean and dressed. Norma has worked hard during our four decades plus of marriage. My mother-in-law did even more during her fifty plus years of matrimony, if that seems possible. She deserves accolades. If you are not certain whether the "she" in the previous sentence refers to my wife or my mother-in-law, take your pick. Either is correct.

When our children became old enough to help with chores, Norma and I carefully outlined their responsibilities so each child had daily, weekly, and monthly chores. Our four children cleaned their rooms, straightened up the rest of the house, did the dishes, washed the cars, maintained the yard, and even watched over the family finances, including writing the checks.

After the children married and moved out, Norma and I resumed our responsibilities along the original lines. Some would call them strict, sexist, and unpleasant. Since we have been in semiretirement much of that has changed.

We now live on an acreage in Iowa. Norma loves to ride our small, tractor-type lawnmower, and she cuts most of the grass — over an acre of it. Mowing is usually a twice-a-week job in the summer. For years I've often helped with the dishes, and I usually vacuum the carpets. Still, I share only a small part of the total workload.

Her retirement income is also greater than mine at present. Though this fact doesn't bother me now, it might have a few decades ago. Okay, so it still does a little. The point is our views and responsibilities have definitely changed over the years. They resemble the description of "the old gray mare."

Our two sons enjoy cooking. According to their testimony, they do a significant portion of the housework. Whether their wives agree that they carry their share of the load may be another story. But what we've known as "traditional roles" are changing. They will likely shift even more if our society survives. Men presently define with great difficulty what makes them men, husbands, or family heads. On the other side, it may be equally as challenging for women to understand what their roles are.

Discuss candidly in your premarital counseling the various household tasks and how the partners view them. In other words, will doing the dishes or having to change the baby's diapers threaten the husband's masculinity? If the wife earns more than he, will his ego endure it? Don't leave counseling concerning these details unattended until after the wedding.

HOW THE HUSBAND FILLS HIS ROLE AS HEAD

I believe the Scriptures teach that husbands should head families. Defining how they can fill that obligation in a Christlike manner may be one of the greatest challenges we face in this decade. Families suffer, and marriages fail because husbands don't know how to do this. Moreover, male spouses have decreasing numbers of role models.

It's for good reason that the husband should be the head of the family. I've never seen a wife who respected a husband who let her dominate him. Neither have I seen many well adjusted children come from homes where the wife controlled the relationship. Any time a husband defers to his wife because he fears her reaction or simply to avoid a confrontation, we find the potential for miserable spouses and children. But then neither should wives have to cower and fear confrontation with their husbands.

Marriages where the husband tries to rule by invoking authority, or by brutality, are torturous relationships. Jesus led his church by giving his life for it and humbly following the Father. Most of the wives I have counseled would gladly have submitted to a husband who followed Jesus' example.

Many counselors advise couples toward a fifty-fifty relationship. Couples definitely need to discuss issues and decisions, but the spouse with greater verbal skills usually predominates in these situations. Usually wives excel in this department, causing their mates to withdraw resentfully. One old professor of mine pointed out another drawback of the so-called shared leadership or fifty-fifty relationship. "No one ever lives up to his/her part of the bargain," he said. "What usually results is 25% he, 25% she, and 50% fighting." Even when the issue seems resolved by a couple, it doesn't necessarily stay settled. Circumstances constantly present new trials.

I suffer from diabetes. Due to insulin reactions, there are short periods of time that I'm incapable of taking care of myself. My behavior often turns infantile. I'm glad Norma patiently endures those times. But she couldn't respect me if I didn't attempt to lead in my more lucid moments. The approach to the other we both find most refreshing is when each of us affirms the godliness and gifts of the other, bearing patiently when the other lapses into unlovely actions. I'm deeply in arrears to Norma in this department. My debt to her resembles the national one.

Is the Bible simply dated here, deficient in its advice for couples who both work 40-80 hours a week and need to share duties simply to survive? Isn't it only fair that husbands carry their share of the drudgery? It is. But if husbands find themselves sharing in all responsibilities, including dishes and diaper changing, how can they possibly lead their families?

Aren't leaders usually out in front somewhere beyond the ordinary, ugly grunt tasks? That's the typical management perspective. People practiced it in Jesus' day. But Jesus himself didn't buy it. In Jesus' Kingdom, polite servants will eventually get to do the slam-dunking.

Malachi's choice of the word "companion" or "partner" to refer to the "wife of your youth" in the passage previously noted is enough to make male chauvinists shake. In every Old Testament occurrence but this one, the word refers to a close male companion or partner, whether good or bad. The connotation of partnership is there. In case some might wonder, it's never suggestive of two male sexual partners.

Yet when Paul insisted in Ephesians that fathers be the heads, doesn't that intimate that they were in charge of something? It does. Fathers need to be in command of one special area. Most men I know fail miserably in that department. Their brothers have defaulted there for millennia.

In what sphere of duty do most men falter? It's in leading their families in the Lord. In most families, wives show examples of faithfulness by encouraging the family to attend church services, observe family devotions, and prayers at mealtime. Nearly all men I know lapse seriously here. "I stopped attending Sunday school when I was eleven," a father of two children told me recently.

Many sons attend services until about 10-12 years of age. Then seeing the example of their fathers, they perceive that it isn't "manly" to be an active Christian. After that, sons attend church services and lead prayers at family meals with increasing reluctance. Sons and daughters need to see fathers who gladly lead in the Lord.

Having fathers show the way spiritually would likely resolve many problems in the leadership of churches as well as families. Over the past five years, I've served as a guest minister in churches of numerous denominations. Women are taking increasing roles of leadership in most of those churches. "That's healthy," some would say. Shouldn't women play more prominent roles?

Let's let the women who assume these positions of leadership answer. Most of them I talk with deplore what has happened because they lead by default. Men have simply yielded more ground of leadership. Is it true that they don't have time, or are they possibly ashamed of showing open interest in the Lord? Deborah led ancient Israel because most of the contemporary men developed puniness. Included in the weak group was Judge Shamgar, who had once slain six hundred Philistines with an oxgoad (Judges 3:31; 5:6).

THE EFFECTS ON CHILDREN

Children suffer from the effects of observing wilted fathers in the same way they suffer from abusive parents. I recall a teenaged girl who came to my office lamenting: "Mom will never let Dad win an argument." She resented her mother for the domination of her father. She was angry with her father for allowing it to happen. Review with the couple their plans for bringing children into the world, and how they will make decisions regarding their families.

Paul followed Old Testament precedent when he charged fathers in Ephesus to bring up their children in the "training and instruction of the Lord" (Ephesians 6:4). To what Old Testament example do I refer? Israelite dads were instructed to explain why they observed Passover and other ordinances (Deuteronomy 6:4-9). Now, in order for society to regain sanity and balance, fathers must assume responsibility for leading their families in the Lord.

When husbands/fathers use Christian principles to lead their families, it lessens the likelihood of disruptive problems. I recall one family in which the father was selfishly career oriented. His young son's behavior imaged the father's power-seeking, demanding attitude. The wife/mother caved in to both in futility. Then the father became a disciple of Jesus and began changing his life. He led his family in the Lord. The wife gained new hope as she saw the changes the Lord wrought in her husband. They both found help in the Scriptures to discipline the son properly. He became far more lovable and controllable. Even I enjoyed being around him.

REVIEWING PARENTAL ROLES

Review with your candidates their ideas on disciplining children. It's helpful to relate several "what-if" situations to note how they would react. These might include: Do the candidates agree on the type of discipline to administer? If they disagree, whose ideas will prevail? Will their disagreements be handled in such a way that their children can't play upon or be hurt by their disunity? Do they agree that their children will receive increasing amounts of responsibility as they mature? How will they handle choices regarding friendships their children may form? Do they share views on the place of faith, prayer, and religion in their lives? Do they agree on what they will teach their children concerning right and wrong?

If there are stepchildren involved, does the natural parent feel comfortable allowing the stepparent to discipline? Do the natural and stepchildren concerned have a clear understanding of how disciplining will be administered and by whom? Do the candidates agree on whether to have children, and the number?

A Look at Finances

Disagreements over finances are a major cause of divorce. Does the candidate couple agree on how to spend their income? The choices available to us now create noxious niches where the devil loves to hang out. The type of home to purchase or whether they see the purchase of a home as an option needs thorough discussion. How they view the use of credit and what purchases should have priority require attention as well. Plastic homes rarely house persisting unions.

I think it wise to interview the potential spouses individually on matters such as these. Note any differences so you can discuss them jointly later. Why do I say this? I've reviewed such concerns many times with candidates as they sat holding hands in my office. They seemed in starry-eyed agreement on everything that we discussed. Later, to my chagrin, I discovered that one had simply yielded to the dominating prince or princess charming.

The Candidates' Views of Sex and Morality

Simply because a couple sits comfortably, almost ecstatically, in your office doesn't mean that they will automatically find satisfaction fifty years later. It doesn't even guarantee it on their wedding night. Their views of sex, their standards of morality, and what those standards are based on, require serious attention.

Discuss birth control. Include in your counseling sessions a review of the following questions: Do they concur on its need? Do they agree on the methods to be used? Have they consulted a physician concerning the risks of each method?

Making Holidays Happy Days

When Norma and I first got married, one of the biggest sources of conflict for us was where to spend holidays. Although my parents had little to spend when I was a child, holidays were important family days. So were birthdays. Because Norma and I moved about fifteen hundred miles from both parents, we spent our first Christmas needing each other. But by our second Christmas, we were within ten miles of both sets of parents and in the midst of controversy.

Inability to resolve these issues causes life-lasting hard feelings among couples and their families. We resolved the problem for ourselves when we moved a thousand miles away and began establishing family traditions for our own children. Cover this ground over the river and through the woods with marriage candidates. The give and take they exhibit on this subject will give you early warning of whether they can expect holiday greetings or grief.

Discussing these issues helps them and you learn how candidly they express their feelings. Our intent is to show how important it is to develop a personal relationship with Jesus, and to pattern our lives after his example. Submitted lives make stormy days calmer and rainy days shorter. They also rear offspring that tend to shock and jolt the world less.

To help the couple grow together in the Lord, suggest that they begin praying together at the beginning of the day or at the close. Keep on hand an updated bibliography of works on various aspects of the subject of Christian marriage. Then you can easily refer the couple to tracts, manuals, or other publications that they will find helpful. I recommend suggesting materials that aren't too lengthy or wordy unless you know that the candidates are avid readers.

Chapter Two

GOALS FOR THE
MARRIAGE SERVICE

THE IMPORTANCE OF GOAL CLARIFICATION

If the officiant uses the proper ritual, shouldn't everything else fall into order? After all, good churchmen designed most wedding rituals centuries ago. Why do we need goals in respect to the service?

In my first several months of ministry in Hollywood, proving that I could successfully serve as a minister was extremely important to me. I wanted to demonstrate success in the Kingdom by baptizing people into Christ. I eagerly sought new converts.

One Sunday during the invitation, a man in his fifties strode forward. I had spent time talking and studying with him the previous week. He was converting from a major non-Christian religion. Happy as I was to see someone added to the body of Christ, and though eager to impress my elders, congregation, and peers, something about his demeanor as he approached bothered me. It seemed as if he came, not humbly, but proudly, maybe arrogantly. I questioned his purposes and his heart that day. I think I had good reason. As is evident to you, I should have questioned my own motivation, too.

Here's my point. I could have baptized the man that Sunday according to biblical form and the accepted manner of the Church. It would have impressed my elders, the congregation, and my peers. I'm not sure it would have pleased God. Neither did my motivation that day please him. He looks for right motives, honorable purposes.

That's why we need to ask questions about the wedding service, whether we conduct it using long established ritual or completely impromptu, whether held on a grand scale or in miniature gauge. The florist, tuxedo shop personnel, and bridal store owners will probably ask no questions beyond "Is your credit card good for this?" But as servants of Jesus we need to ask some sober questions. Which?

How Will This Marriage Service Honor the Lord?

Many couples wish to write their own vows and design their orders of service. You will want to see the wording and be fully informed of all the activities. Some couples flaunt their disdain of Christian values.

I've performed numerous ceremonies for couples young and old in our community. Many of them weren't members of our church. During the sixties, a friend told me that one of our mutual friends planned to ask me to officiate at a wedding for him and his fiancée. I knew him and his family well. He had been an Eagle Scout, but in his late teens he became a free spirit.

The friend said that this young man and his fiancée were considering whether to ask me to perform a ceremony for them in the buff — they, not I. They probably used the friend to broach the subject with me. I scotched it quickly. They never asked.

On another occasion I faced a far more difficult decision. A former member and close friend asked me to perform the marriage service for him and the woman he was dating. My friend was a widower; I had officiated at his first wife's funeral. He moved out of the area for some time, then returned and brought his friend, a divorcée, to services with him on a regular basis. I've performed marriage services for divorced persons after satisfying myself about certain principles. I queried my friend first about the propriety of his relationship. He expressed confidence that God approved.

I told my friend that I wanted to talk with his fiancée before I made my final decision. In our discussion, I learned she had no biblically valid reason for her divorce. Her ex-husband had been completely faithful to her, was hardworking, responsible, and still loved her. I declined to perform the ceremony. I lost a friend for a while. He married the woman anyway. The marriage lasted about a year ending in a costly divorce — expensive emotionally and financially.

Now I feel that I could have handled the situation with greater sensitivity. The misunderstanding between us might have been avoided. I love and respect my friend. Nonetheless, no persuasion could have convinced me that his union to that woman honored God. As deeply as I regret the pain that I possibly caused, I believe my remorse today would be greater had I given approbation to that marriage.

In some cases, I caved in weakly to pressure to officiate at marriage services about which I had strong doubts. For those my conscience pains me, and I ask God's forgiveness.

CAN THE COUPLE AFFORD THE SERVICE?

Every Spring a nearby, small town newspaper features a section on weddings. It's likely supported by the local businesses associated with nuptials. The segment this year lists all the items necessary for a proper wedding in this rural community. The list includes flowers, gowns, announcements, parties, etc. The cost of these "necessary" items runs into thousands of dollars. What most couples appear to spend seems excessive considering the average income of the people in the community.

In 1990, in the U.S., the average bridal dress cost about $800. That didn't include the veil. A typical head covering ran another $170. Add the necessary undergarments, shoes, headpieces, and other accessories, to say nothing of flowers, chapels, limousines, cakes, banquets, bands (rings and musical), photographers, bridal advisers, and most couples and families understand that the "poorer" applies to them, and "richer" applies to the associated businesses.

These extraordinary expenses often become the source of anguish that erupts between the couple and their families. At times, all the arrangements have been made before the couple gets to the minister. In a few instances, the families can afford it and are glad to spend it. In most cases, the planners incur substantial debt for this "once in a lifetime occasion." We should counsel couples whenever we can to stick with responsible, realistic planning.

Ask if they have consulted with each other and with their parents on how much funding is available. Advise them to tailor everything else to that cost. Their willingness to do this strongly indicates how maturely they relate to each other and to their parents. If they don't agree to this, you may want to extend the period of counseling for them. Otherwise prepare your extinguishers for family fire and ire.

Do the Parties Agree on the Type of Service?

Some years ago, a young couple that Norma and I know well planned their marriage service. They understood the financial constraints and wanted a wedding attended only by family and close friends. The prospective bride and groom were both shy. They dreaded the pressure of a large event. Both sets of parents were more socially active. When speaking with the couple they would say, "But if you invite the Jones family, you also have to invite the Smiths." Soon the invitation list tripled. One weekend a few months prior to the announced date of the marriage, the couple called to say that they were in Las Vegas. They were on their way to a wedding chapel and wanted their parents' blessing. If you suspect that this may be a problem, meet at least once with both sets of parents and the couple to see if they are listening to one another and considering the feelings and needs of each person.

What Should a Scriptural Service Accomplish?

1. The couple should understand that they are answerable to God, and that they will recite their vows before him.

Traditional rituals usually emphasize this. However, three factors work strongly against cognitive perception of this during the ceremony. One, many rituals use archaic language that seems unreal and unfamiliar to persons conditioned to modern vernacular. Two, the wording has been heard so many times by the participants that they no longer receive its impact. Three, the wedding party members usually find themselves preoccupied with stage fright, concerns about how they look, and wondering about who is present. Few words penetrate the make-up, tears, and tuxedos.

These factors make it important to emphasize early in the counseling sessions the need to honor God first, and how serious the vows are. I discovered that earnest communication must take place from the first. In the week prior to the wedding, all the parties, with the exception of the groom, get totally immersed in wedding details and activities. He tends to think about the honeymoon.

How much does understanding the importance of those vows matter? My wife and I realized how much on a few occasions many years ago. It was only those vows that we said before God that kept us together. We're extremely glad for that last adhesive shred. Too many couples find that in times of conflict no lasting binder remains.

2. The marriage service makes public testimony that a new family has been formed.

It's important that the parents understand the meaning of Genesis 2:24, "For this reason a man will leave his father and mother and be united to his wife, and they will become one flesh." Children need to always honor their parents, but after the marriage ceremony the couple are one flesh. They need to give each other the highest priority.

When the parents give their daughter away during the ceremony, it signifies that they give up their hold on her. The parents of the groom should also understand that their son is now a part of a separate family unit comprised of the new bride and groom. A mother whose daughter married and moved across the country complained that she never got to see her daughter anymore. "She can always get a husband, but she has only one mother!" she grumbled. Impress on both sets of parents that their children "leave" them when they get married.

3. The ceremony says to friends and associates, "This man and woman now pledge their fidelity to each other." It signals to all those who might still have eyes for the bride or groom, "Hands off."

4. Ceremonies should be public statements of cooperation and fellowship of the families. This may not always be possible, but I believe the minister needs to do everything "by prayer and supplication" to bring it about.

5. The ceremony should enhance the beauty of the bride and the handsomeness of the husband.

Here we must be sensitive to how cultural conditioning affects us. You and the couple may have to consult on what is tasteful and appropriate. The Old Testament Song of Songs (or Song of Solomon) emphasizes the attractiveness of the bride and groom: "Most beautiful of women" (S. of S. 1:8), and "How handsome you are, my lover!" (S. of S. 1:16). John saw the "new Jerusalem, coming down out of heaven from God, prepared as a bride beautifully dressed for her husband" (Revelation 21:2). Charming weddings appear to please the Lord.

6. It's a time of celebration.

Song of Songs also reflects celebration. "Flowers appear on the earth; the season of singing has come" (S. of S. 2:12). I began to appreciate how beautiful the spirit of celebration can be for couples and their families after attending some Jewish weddings. Too few of the Christian services that I've witnessed proclaim this. Although it's important to underscore the seriousness of the vows, we don't have to act as though we're angry, scared, or agitated.

In addition to the example of Solomon in his Song, other reasons make it prudent to make the service a time of celebration that includes humor. Most listeners can endure serious conversation by a speaker for about seven minutes. Communication malfunctions after that. Humor helps concentration. It doesn't need to be rollicking and certainly not sordid, but its presence is almost as necessary as the bride's is.

For those who base their rejection of humor on the fact that a wedding is a worship service, I cite Nehemiah 8. The chapter describes a sobering moment in the history of Israel. The exiles have just returned from many years of captivity brought on by faithless disobedience. They come home penitent and submissive. Verse six describes how they bowed, "and worshiped the LORD with their faces to the ground." Ezra stood before them with the Book of the Law of God. As he read, those assisting him explained it to the people. The law, of course, reminded them of their waywardness and desperate situation. They wept. Ezra, Nehemiah, and the Levites advised them, "Do not mourn or weep."

But the leaders gave more than just a negative command. In verse ten, Governor Nehemiah ordered, "Go and enjoy choice food and sweet drinks, and send some to those who have nothing prepared. This day is sacred to our Lord. Do not grieve, for the joy of the LORD is your strength."

According to Deuteronomy 16:9-12, Israel also rejoiced and celebrated during the Feast of Weeks (Pentecost). Last, but hardly least, humor helps set people at ease.

7. The marriage service sets a mood of honor, forgiveness, and love, which should last as long as the couple lives. Achieving that mood is one of our tasks. It's therefore necessary that we speak and act consistent with that objective.

8. The ceremony should help the couple feel married.

The message and the medium must be joined to help the couple feel that they indeed have entered a new life together. Length of the ceremony, dignity, and ritual all help to accomplish this.

If the candidates and their families don't agree on these goals, consider blowing your retreat bugle. Otherwise you may get buried beside General Custer at the Little Bighorn. The old proverb that starts, "Fools rush in . . ." describes too much of my ministry. Jesus didn't attempt to solve every problem for those who approached him. When encountering persons motivated by greed, he declined to become involved. Recall the man in Luke 12:13 who asked Jesus to intercede with his brother to obtain a share of the inheritance. The Lord refused to become entangled. I pray for more of his wisdom and discernment. It would have saved me many scars.

Chapter Three

TYPES OF MARRIAGE SERVICES

DEFINING THE TYPES

Defining wedding types is almost as impossible as describing what a dog looks like. One of our sons and his wife own a Yorkshire terrier. One of our daughters and her husband enjoy two slobbery Newfoundlands. Stormy, the terrier, barely weighs three pounds. We step gingerly in her presence. One misstep and she's a canine Rorschach. Rocky, the male Newfoundland, weighs about 150 pounds. Around him we worry about being the Rorschach.

The two breeds of dog don't share hair color, head shape, or dispositions. Telling someone not familiar with the species what a dog looks like presents one with considerable difficulty. So does defining wedding types. Therefore, our definitions include broad categories.

Factors affecting definition include: setting, number of persons involved, the attire of the celebrants and guests, length, location, wording of the service, and content of the vows. Even the types of invitations affect the definition.

Geography, culture, and personal preference create crossovers between categories further complicating our definitions. Therefore the categories listed below are not rigid. They may be gelatinous.

FOUR GENERAL CATEGORIES

Very formal or classic

The guest list usually exceeds three hundred, all of whom will be treated to a sit-down luncheon or dinner. Because of the number of guests, at least six ushers are required. The rule of thumb is one for each fifty guests. The wedding party also will likely include one or two flower girls, a ring bearer, and possibly a trainbearer, all in appropriate attire.

The bride will wear a gown with a long train and full veil; the groom will be attired in black tie. If the event is held after six p.m., the groom wears white tie. All guests wear equivalent formal attire. Invitations are formal, and usually engraved.

Formal, including military

The formal wedding is generally what we envision when we think about traditional weddings. The bride usually adorns herself with a long wedding dress and veil. The bridesmaids wear floor-length gowns. Guests dress up, but not necessarily in formal wear. Grooms and ushers wear tuxedos or dinner jackets. The guest list may vary from one hundred to two hundred fifty. There should be at least one usher for each fifty guests. There may be an equivalent number of bridesmaids.

Military weddings — Service men and women are entitled to have military services. These are formal occasions with all military persons in full dress including white gloves. Brides in the military may wear either their dress uniforms or bridal gowns.

Ushers seat military guests in order of rank. Military personnel should know how to do this. It's best for those planning the wedding to consult the officer in charge of protocol at the academy of whichever service(s) may be involved. At the conclusion of the marriage service, it is traditional for the bride and groom to pass under the arch of swords or sabers, swords if navy, sabers if army. This ceremony is available to officers only. Usually four to six bearers are involved. They may also serve as ushers. If you are located near a base, a chaplain may be able to inform you of the particulars. Be sure to plan well in advance.

Semiformal

At a semiformal wedding the bride can wear a long or a short gown. Some experts on etiquette say she shouldn't wear a veil unless the wedding is held in the evening. She may if she wishes; it's her wedding. She may prefer to wear a headpiece, hat, or floral wreath. Her attendants likely will wear colorful dresses the same length or shorter than hers. Usually not more than two persons attend the bride. The men generally wear dark suits all of one color. The guest list runs fifty to one hundred persons.

Informal

This style refers to those ceremonies that only relatives and close friends attend. The guest list rarely exceeds fifty persons. The bride wears a street length dress or suit and others dress accordingly.

Double weddings — Siblings or friends who are close may ask you some day to perform a double wedding. These occasions presumably save families expense and duplication of the ordeal. If it appears in your interviews that the parties and parents concerned favor it, and you detect no jealousy or resentment, it may be safe to proceed with caution. On the other hand, you might consider the Lord's advice to Job about wrestling the Leviathan (often identified with the crocodile), "Think of the battle; you will not do it again!" (Job 41:8, RSV).

Okay, so you are going to do it anyway. Here are a few suggestions regarding protocol.

Invitations: If the brides are sisters, they usually issue the invitations jointly.

Attendants: Frequently one couple acts as maid of honor and best man for the other. Other attendants are chosen separately.

Attire: Brides should wear similar gowns or dresses. One shouldn't try to outdo the other. If they wish, they can have their attendants wear different colors. The colors should be complementary, however.

Who goes first? Generally the elder goes first. When there are two aisles they can walk simultaneously. The two sets of ushers begin the procession followed by the bridal attendants, ring bearer, flower girl, and the first bride. Next come the second set of attendants and the bride. The grooms follow the minister in side by side, their best men following. During the recessional, the elder bride and her groom go first.

Who gives the brides away? If sisters prefer, their father can walk between them, or they can have mother and father escort them, or father and brother.

Where to stand: The attendants of the first bride usually stand on the left and her husband-to-be stands nearer the aisle.

The order: If the vows are not done simultaneously, proceed with those of the elder sister first. If the brides aren't sisters and aren't in agreement as to who should go first, it might be fairest to follow biblical precedent and cast lots.

Receiving lines: If the brides are sisters, only one receiving line is necessary. Otherwise use two separate lines. This is suggested protocol. If both brides agree, they may use any order that they and you deem appropriate.

INTERVIEWING THE COUPLE

Some couples come with carefully prepared plans. Others bring only vague ideas complicated considerably by input from a potpourri of sources. Keeping in mind the goals we've established, we need to review with the couple what type of ceremony they envision. At the same time, consider expenses and available facilities.

Discuss your fee or honorarium. I didn't charge members of our church. On occasion I returned money they offered me. I know peers who never charge. They reason that the church pays them adequately. It's proper etiquette to graciously accept what is offered. In most cases, considering the extra time and energy expended, the honoraria are trifling. Sometimes I waived the fee for nonmembers. They were poor, yet living responsibly; I wanted to encourage them. I think it's wise to consider the financial condition of the couple.

Years ago while I was having Sunday lunch with several members of our church, attention was directed to a bachelor member/friend in his mid-thirties. He had been dating a young woman in the congregation. All of us believed they were well matched, but Perry was extremely slow in asking for Polly's hand. Several of us at the table offered various inducements for him to set the date within six months. An M.D. offered free medical care for any children born. I volunteered to perform the ceremony gratis, and even made an agreement with a mutual friend that one of us would buy the license for the couple.

Perry called a few days later to inform me that they had set the date — five days prior to the deadline given him. As it turned out, I also had to purchase the license. Perry, my good New England friend, even made me accompany them to the courthouse. In the interim, the fee had tripled. Would I do that again? Without question. Perry and Polly remain among our closest friends and have three wonderful children.

APPROPRIATE APPAREL FOR YOU

Once the type of wedding is resolved, you will need to discuss the appropriate attire for you. Will your vestments be suitable? Will your colors cause a mismatch? I don't use robes. I nearly always wear a black suit. But all my ties have Mickey Mouse on them somewhere. A couple for whom I performed a ceremony in Southern California a few years ago, decided on black and red as their colors because the ceremony was to be held at Christmas time. They feared I wouldn't have the proper colored tie. They purchased a bright red Mickey Mouse tie for me. Now I have an assortment of reds and about every other color.

A friend who graduated in the seventies from the University of California, Santa Barbara, made the most unusual apparel request I ever accepted. We held the ceremony in the backyard of a home overlooking the Pacific Ocean. Mountains covered with avocado and eucalyptus trees surrounded it.

Joelle wore a beautiful gown. Mike dressed in a handsome suit, but he wanted to be the only person present wearing one. He requested that I wear a sport shirt. I agreed readily. As

Norma and I put our clothes into the car for the trip from Hollywood to Santa Barbara, it shocked her to learn I wasn't taking my "marrying and burying suit."

My lack of clerical apparel caused embarrassment later. The guests were all seated in the yard. One important guest was late in arriving, however. Mike and Joelle didn't want to begin without him. The couple was to enter from separate directions. I was to come in from a third. My path took me behind the garage so I could join them in the yard. I waited in the kitchen, biding my time watching for the late guest.

The mutual friends who owned the residence hired a young woman to assist them with arrangements. She looked at me probably wondering about the nondescript character loitering in the kitchen. I assumed she knew my identity. I commented to her, "Maybe we can get this wedding started shortly." She tartly responded, "Sir, if you'll go take your seat, I'm sure we can."

One caution. Many of us in ministry have a tendency to show off. I think it best that we not outdo the bride and groom; we should allow them to be the real stars. This became especially evident when my wife and I attended a service in San Diego some years ago. It was a garden setting. We had never met the bride, only the groom. Suddenly a woman appeared wearing a stunning white suit. We assumed she was the bride. She was not. She was the minister. Next to her the bride looked drab.

While you discuss the type of clothing each one is to wear, resolve what type of garb you and they will wear at rehearsal. There is a present trend toward informality.

MUSIC AND SPECIAL EFFECTS

Find out early in your interviews what types of music the couple plans to use. Will they have soloists? Do they expect to use piano, organ, guitar, etc., or prerecorded music? If they wish to use nonchurch instruments, when will the musicians set up, and can the building accommodate the speakers and other parts of the sound system?

Is the music in keeping with Christian worship services and the seriousness of the couple's vows? Does it accord with the joy of celebration? Unpleasant surprises can create terrible mood swings in officiants rendering them unsuitable for leading in worship, especially this officiant.

Chapter Four

LEGAL REQUIREMENTS
AND YOUR PREPARATION

WHO MAY PERFORM CEREMONIES

In most states, judges of courts, justices of the peace, notaries of the public, and ordained or recognized clergypersons qualify to perform ceremonies. It's possible that mayors of cities and governors have the authority to perform marriage rites in some states. Apparently ships' captains no longer qualify. Did too many tugboat captains abuse the office?

Requirements vary concerning the clergy. Check with the department responsible for this in your local county courthouse. In years past, Oregon required ministers to be ordained. California law specifies only that they be recognized ministers of a church.

Don't be amazed if you find no one in your local county courthouse that can inform you with certainty about current laws. Pursue the matter until you find someone who can speak with expertise. I don't know how often the legality of marriages is challenged on the basis of the officiant's lack of qualification, but it's best not to be the test case.

Denominations differ, too, on requirements for ordination. In Churches of Christ, we have no ordination ceremonies. My ordination to satisfy the state of Oregon was not easily obtained. The local elders of the church where I preached for a time in the late 1950s had absolutely no experience with ordination and balked at my first request.

Who May Get Married

Your denomination may specify restrictions on the age of persons and the eligibility of divorced persons. Churches of Christ have no written creeds, ordinances, or national headquarters. We are ostensibly free, though unwritten creeds, as some of us have discovered, can be just as binding as the ones on printed pages. I simply try to follow the principles the New Testament gives. Admittedly this leaves areas of differing interpretations.

Legal ages of applicants for marriage licenses also vary widely. This information is vital. Performing a ceremony for an underage person in some states could presumably make you an accessory to statutory rape.

If during your interviews you suspect that a previous marriage hasn't been terminated, you may want to ask for documentation. Better yet, you may want to retreat. Recently there was an article in the local paper about a woman in South Dakota who had married three different men. She had divorced none of them. The courts are now trying to determine which man gets to keep her.

What Records You Should Keep

After performing each ceremony, I make a copy of the license and file it. I keep a separate file for each service labeled with the couple's name. I do this for several reasons. First, the mail service on which we depend to deliver the signed copy of the license is not totally reliable.

Second, in busy counties such as Los Angeles County, the licenses are stuffed into a huge drawer to await recording, thus going through several hands. To my knowledge, no license I returned was lost, but it's possible some couple out there presumes they are legally married and the documents may not be on file to prove it.

Third, I keep a copy of the service materials so I'll know what I've said and done on each occasion. When you continue performing wedding services in the same locality and before many of the same people, it helps to use different stories and illustrations.

I also record in the file the amount of the honorarium I received; I note it in my appointment book, too. The IRS may want verification some day. If you use a computer, you may record things differently. The important thing is to have some reliable system for retaining and recalling information.

WHAT THE LAW REQUIRES OF THE COUPLE

Ordinarily the couple applies in person at the appropriate office. This may be the marriage license bureau or the county recorder. Nomenclature and the departments responsible for this vary widely from state to state.

The legal age varies, too. Underage persons may need parental or even court approval. Some states require waiting periods. Most insist on blood tests. If your county prints brochures giving the necessary information, obtain several copies for your file that you can give to couples making inquiry of you.

Usually the couple brings the license issued by the county to the ceremony. Once the ceremony is performed, the minister signs as the officiant, has the witnesses sign, and then returns the completed document to the appropriate agency. This may or may not be the same department that originally issued it.

In California, a confidential type of license that doesn't require a blood test can be issued to couples who have been cohabiting for a specified length of time. California law also allows ministers to draw up a document for cohabiting couples and to file it. No license is necessary. I never exercised that option.

WHAT CONSTITUTES A LEGAL CEREMONY

The following are requirements for a legal ceremony in most states: Does each partner accept the other in matrimony? The officiant must state the basis for his/her authority to perform the ceremony, i.e., as a Minister of the Gospel. The proper number of persons must witness the ceremony.

Your denomination possibly requires certain things of you and the couple. Familiarize yourself with these prior to the first inquiry that may be made of you.

THE USE OF FORMS

Time and frustration can be saved through the use of forms. They also help you to cover areas often overlooked if you depend on your memory alone. It's easier to coordinate building usage, too. This avoids conflicts with others who may contemplate using the building at the same time, e.g., youth groups, singles, women, and community groups.

Make two separate forms available for the couple when they first make their request. The first form is an application to have you officiate at the service. Information should include: names, addresses, parents' names and addresses, phone numbers, religious affiliation, ages, how long they have known each other, any previous marriages, whether they are agreeable to premarital counseling, when they can make themselves available for counseling, social security numbers, site of proposed wedding, dates and times of proposed wedding and rehearsals, and number of bridal attendants. (See the sample form at the end of the book.)

Provide a separate form for them to apply to use the church building. Although a sample form is printed in the back of the book, you should consult a tax attorney before you use it. Tax laws vary from state to state in respect to nonprofit organizations. The Internal Revenue Service raises questions about tax exempt status when church buildings are rented. Your state taxing agency might also.

Other reasons make it beneficial to use forms. When we are organized it saves us time. If you or your secretary, or the janitor for that matter, can quickly pull a form out of the file or from the computer, you may free yourself for other tasks.

Businesslike approaches make good first impressions when couples call on us. They help hasten the couples' development of confidence in us if we appear professional and prepared at our first meeting.

SUGGESTIONS ON THE USE OF FORMS

1) Maintain a church calendar through which all events are cleared.

2) Keep application forms in the church office so the church secretary can distribute them to all parties concerned. Church building availability can be verified at the time of distribution.

3) Ask for promptness from the couple in keeping their appointments, and set a good example for them.

4) Have sample marriage services and vows on hand to give to the couple at the first interview in the event you agree to officiate.

5) Have a policy statement on file to review with or to hand the couple regarding your wishes concerning photographers, videotaping, etc. I permit *nonflash* photography if it's unobtrusive.

REGARDING FEES

1) Discuss your fee or honorarium policy candidly.

2) Also include in the building fee or suggested donation, ample amounts to pay to open and close the building, and for preparation and clean up for rehearsal and wedding. Include, if necessary, payment for operating the sound system, special lighting, and for persons to be available when flowers are delivered and the candelabra, floral baskets, etc., are picked up afterward.

3) If your church does not already have a policy concerning building usage for members and nonmembers, you may want to urge the board to set one. Clear policy statements help avoid the appearance of favoritism.

Chapter Five

PREMARITAL COUNSELING

DETERMINING COMPATIBILITY

Only the Lord knows with certainty whether a couple can live in harmony and love for a lifetime. I feel increasingly less capable of predicting success for others, although I'm thankful that a good percentage of the couples I had the honor to help remains happily married.

Numerous psychological tests and profiles are available to determine compatibility. I advise checking with your colleagues for their recommendations. A few of my peers in Southern California wouldn't officiate unless the couple agreed to take the tests. If you feel unqualified to administer them, and you suspect some potential problem, refer the couple to a certified counselor. One question to face is, What will you do if the tests reveal severe incompatibility?

In later years, I have used a personal Bible study that helps identify areas of weakness and potential problems. The study is not in print. It can't be, because it must be learned in real life settings. The study focuses on what behaviors the Lord expects us to quit once we wear his name. The lessons make good use of passages like Galatians 5:19-26, Romans 1, and 1 Corinthians 6:9-20. They also emphasize the positive qualities necessary for enduring marriages.

Some problems we identify in compatibility testing should cause us to raise yellow flags on the marriage track. Discovering addictions to alcohol, drugs, gambling, greed, possessiveness, selfishness, and adultery should incite red flags.

LOOKING FOR GUARANTEES OF SUCCESS?

Some marital researchers claim they can predict with greater than 90 percent accuracy which married couples will stay married.[1] Roofers often give 30 year warranties on their work. I have a feeling that most would rather sign the contract with an older person than a young one. But guarantees of marriage compatibility, regardless of what any test or profile might reveal, are as dangerous as a Titanic with Custer in command. Why do I say that?

First, the dynamics of life make permanent resolution of any problem impossible. In 1 Corinthians 10:12, Paul warned against thinking that we can relegate all problems to the past tense. Every married person experiences fickle feelings. One day we may feel totally in love with our spouse, the next day totally annoyed.

Second, you have probably known couples who seem destined for each other. They enjoyed hobbies and activities together, came from similar cultures, and shared the same religion. It appeared that they would sail the love boat forever. Almost without warning you see them paddling in opposite courses away from their capsized ship. Other couples appear to share little in common yet somehow prevail in marital felicity.

Not many in our families and among our friends felt confident that Norma and I would remain married. Our families shared few of the same perspectives on life. Even after forty plus years, many of our interests don't parallel. We experienced several stormy periods in the early years. We still find ourselves sharing opposite views on important subjects.

Do couples who have been married for decades share some secret adhesive? Yes and no. Norma and I credit any success to the grace of God. In fact, we were so poor for the first several years neither of us could afford a divorce lawyer. Otherwise,

Norma jokes, she may have departed long ago. We also didn't want to move back home. We both loved our parents, but neither of us wanted to live with them again. Here's what I'm saying. Certain factors can override all others and will work to keep couples together, and even cause growth in their love for each other.

The first of these is the couple's commitment to God and each other. When I said my vows to Norma, I meant to keep them. At times only that thread links couples together. But it's crucial. It stitches our clothes on in the presence of persons we're not wed to.

Second, Norma and I stayed within an environment generally favorable to marriage — the Church. Occasionally, events and situations within the church made us angry with each other. Frequently, persons of both sexes within the church didn't respect their marriage vows or ours. But comparing the relationships within the church with those we would have found outside, it's certain that we were in the environment most conducive to marriage. Every couple needs friends who affirm the sanctity of marriage vows.

Each spouse needs to be in a personal relationship with the Lord. Norma was beautiful when I married her. Her growing respect for God makes her increasingly lovely. When couples make a commitment to God, continue in a favorable Christian environment, and maintain a close relationship with God, the odds of marital success increase — even for odd couples.

DEALING WITH SPECIAL SITUATIONS

Divorced Candidates — Earlier we considered Jesus' teaching on the seriousness of wedding vows. We should divorce with the same willingness that we would give up an arm or a leg. I've known many ministers that absolutely refused to perform marriage services for divorced candidates. Others drew the line at whether the divorced parties had just cause, e.g., had their mates committed adultery?

Hard line policies lead to inconsistencies. "Innocent parties" in some cases of adultery discourage the "guilty" one by withholding sex, a violation of principles found in 1 Corinthians 7.

Living in that situation doesn't excuse the "guilty" one, but the so-called "innocent" party shouldn't be considered blameless.

I try to look at each situation on the basis of maturity attained. Is the divorced candidate now exhibiting evidence of readiness to abide by Christian principles, or simply putting flashy paint on a bent frame with a twisted mind?

Hard line policies also enroll us in the Pharisee school. Those students, according to Jesus, loaded "people down with burdens they can hardly carry, and you yourselves will not lift one finger to help them" (Luke 11:46).

In a given year in this country now there are half as many divorces as new marriages. We place unreasonable burdens on divorced persons, in my opinion, when we expect them to live the rest of their lives in chastity. It's impossible to untangle the snarls people create who neglect God's will. But they can mitigate further muddling by following the teachings of Jesus.

Cohabiting Couples — The incidence of couples living together has risen dramatically since the sixties. It occurs within every age group. My wife and I knew several older couples who lived together in Southern California. Ironically, they were persons considered conservative in other aspects of lifestyle. The phenomenon is not new; the woman at the well in Samaria practiced it in the twenties of the first century A.D. Nonetheless, the wont of people doing it presents special problems for ministers and church leaders today.

My understanding of 1 Corinthians 5 leads me to believe we should place adulterers in two different categories. In that passage, Paul warned Christians to shun fornicators. They were neither to worship with them nor eat with them. But the apostle drew a distinction that Christian teachers often neglect. Paul urged us to disfellowship Christian fornicators, not non-Christian ones. Otherwise, he said, you would have to leave the world. We aren't meant to judge the world, only fellow Christians.

How should we apply the principles Paul gave us? If we discover members of our church living together, we let them know that if they want the continued fellowship of the church, they must live apart until their marriage. Failure to apply this policy leads to a total breakdown of morality in the church. It crumbles the church long before the building itself erodes.

In the case of nonmembers, we try to befriend them so we can teach them about the Lord. Practicing that has given me numerous opportunities to share the good news of life.

Possible Interference from In-laws — Some in-law problems manifest themselves prior to the wedding. Many come about because of insensitive behavior at weddings. Encourage couples to be sympathetic to the needs and feelings of their parents. That's part of the honor due their fathers and mothers. On the other hand, some parents are meddlesome and selfish in their demands.

It helps to identify attitudes toward parents in the first stages of interviewing candidates. In younger couples, one or both may simply want to escape the strictures of home. Marriage seems a convenient route for them. Determine whether the couple carries resentment or hostility toward either set of parents. Their indignation may seem justified, but the baggage of anger, hatred, and bitterness will overload them quickly. Better to delay the wedding until the couple learns forgiveness and appreciation. Gratitude creates warm glows; ingratitude produces glowers.

Frequently the couple has made every effort to make amends and to create peace with their parents. If we find that is true, we should back the children. At all costs we must avoid involvement in bickering and vindictiveness.

Cross-culture, Religion, and Ethnicity — Norma and I are both blue-eyed, fair-haired persons, and we came from Christian homes. We met at church. Presumably we shared the same culture. What an erroneous presumption. Her parents were from Texas, mine from northern states. Norma liked fried okra and cornbread dressing. I preferred the sage dressing my mother prepared. Our family loved to sing, hers didn't. Now I like cornbread dressing, and she loves to sing. But food and family customs became early sources of conflict that nearly separated us.

It isn't always easy to discern the nature of culture, particularly in modern American society. Traditionally, Northern and

Southern cultures differ, and what a vast difference exists between New England and West Coast varieties. How much can these differences affect the future of a marriage? Considerably, unless each partner willingly compromises.

Our society faces an even greater challenge as persons of numerous ethnic groups meet and marry. In the 1990 census, twenty-one percent of the population of Los Angeles was found to be foreign born. In Dade County, Florida, it was eighteen percent. Many marriages are taking place across ethnic and cultural lines. Japanese-Americans marry non-Japanese nearly sixty-five percent of the time. According to the 1990 census Anglos comprise about seventy-five percent of the American population. Some project that by 2050 they will represent about fifty percent. Significant gains are expected in the Latino and Asian sectors. Demographers foresee increasing numbers of couples low-hurdling barriers of culture, ethnicity, and color.[2]

Norma and I probably saw the future in microcosm in Los Angeles. The Lord gave me the privilege of officiating at numerous marriages involving persons of different cultures and races. These changes in customs force two crucial questions. First, does the Bible speak to the issue of intercultural or interethnic marriages in any way? I believe it does.

The Old Testament treats the matter in Numbers 12. Miriam and Aaron criticized Moses because of his Cushite wife. Was she of a different color? The Bible doesn't tell us, although she possibly was darker than Moses was. But she clearly came from a different race and culture.

Miriam's caviling caused a frightening case of leprosy. Fortunately Moses interceded for her healing. Objections to marriage based on racial prejudice appear not to please the Lord. They may bring his judgment.

Yet when couples of differing backgrounds come to us, we wisely advise them to ponder how they will deal with cultural differences. They need also to consider the implications for their offspring. How will they resolve possible conflicts, and how will they handle any isolation the marriage may cause from family and other persons of their race or group?

It may be helpful to refer them to a married couple of similar backgrounds to discuss with them the pros and cons of their experience.

In a few instances early in my ministry, I officiated at marriage services for Christians when they married non-Christians. I vainly hoped that the non-Christian could be influenced. I no longer am comfortable performing such ceremonies and don't recommend officiating at them.

Handicaps and medical problems — After all four of our children were born, I discovered that I had Type I diabetes. Would or should Norma have married me had we known that I would be afflicted? Should we have had children had we known of my condition?

How should we counsel handicapped persons who may come to us wanting us to officiate for them? Our society faces increasingly more complex decisions as the issue of rights for all persons appears to speed down the fast lane in the opposite direction of genetic awareness and scientifically managed lives. I'm thankful that modern medicine has provided the ability for me to live with my diabetes. But the questions arising because of medical and technological advances may cause us to wish we could resurrect Solomon for answers.

We can't deal with the full issue here. Probably no one grasps all the parameters involved. Possibly the best we can do is develop some general principles to help us in our choices. First, unless biblical principles are in violation, I feel we should avoid telling persons with handicaps that they shouldn't marry. This assumes that they are mentally competent and also can take care of their own finances. We should treat them as we do any marital candidates, i.e., we should review how they foresee the resolving of differences, physical or otherwise. If, aware of the potential problems, they act responsibly, and others are not endangered, I am of the opinion they should proceed as they wish.

In relation to AIDS and other sexually transmitted diseases that place other lives in jeopardy, medical consultation is in order. Those of us in ministry face some hard decisions in respect to these matters in the next decade. I still ponder my first encounter with the issue before I even heard the term AIDS.

A local businessman friend struggled with homosexuality. As we studied the Bible together, he decided to live a straight life. He began dating a mutual friend, an attractive young woman in the community. They frequently visited our home together. Prior to our study, he suffered some physical setbacks. He told me confidentially that the doctor had informed him that his immune system had broken down. Shortly after, I heard the term AIDS for the first time.

My dilemma? One of our close friends was dating another close friend who probably suffered from a dreaded disease that might be communicated to her. Should I warn her thus breaking confidence? After considerable prayer, I decided to wait. I reached my decision based on my confidence that they weren't sleeping together. I thought she was not at immediate risk. They broke up within a short time, and he moved out of the area. Were I to face the issue again, I would demand that the person so infected inform the other immediately.

Dealing with Seniors — The median age of the American population progressively rises. People live longer and tend to enjoy better health. This will probably increase the incidence of marriage among more mature persons. Officiating at marriage services for older persons provided me many occasions to share their joy.

Several years ago, a couple in their eighties asked me to officiate at their marriage. It was the bride's first; the groom was a widower. Several of their friends stood up with them for the happy occasion.

A few days after the ceremony, I called on the couple to make what I call a "thousand mile checkup." The new bride greeted me at the door giggling like a schoolgirl. "Come in, I want to share something with you," she said. As I walked into the house, she laughingly continued, "I was so eager to get to the church for the wedding the other day I forgot to put my false teeth in."

In counseling seniors, different sets of concerns present themselves. A major problem we face now isn't parents that disapprove, but children that disapprove. Is the couple ready for that challenge? Merging assets and estates usually requires legal advice. Some older couples feel comfortable drawing prenuptial agreements. Whether done by legal document or not, they definitely need prenuptial agreement.

Mature couples face other questions. Have they made provisions in the event one or both should become disabled? Do they have compatible wills? Are they planning to be buried alongside their first spouse or the present one? All problems don't end at the grave. At the tomb some families have just begun to fight.

Homosexuals — On the basis of trends in court rulings in this country, it's conceivable to me that in the future, Christian ministers may not have a choice as to whether they consent to perform marriages for persons of the same sex. They may be forced to officiate or face charges of discrimination. My understanding of Leviticus 18:22; 20:13; Romans 1:18-32; and 1 Corinthians 6:9-10 leads me to believe that homosexual behavior is wrong. I won't perform marriage services uniting such persons regardless of who might request it or order it. For me it's one of those division points between allegiance to Caesar and to God.

NOTES

1. See *U.S. News & World Report*, February 21, 1994, p. 66.

2. See *Time*, "Special Issue" Fall, 1993, pp. 64, 65.

Chapter Six

ELEMENTS OF
THE CEREMONY

MAKING HOMILIES BIBLICAL

While preparing sermons, I'm strongly tempted to appear learned. When I succumb, I find myself quoting several authorities on marriage. The effect isn't usually erudition, it's obfuscation.

I also worry about creating the correct mood. Scholarship and effect are worthy goals, but we evidence better grasp of our roles when we bring our lessons and ourselves into submission to Jesus.

Strive to make your presentations biblically based. Because we stand accountable to God in acts of worship, all elements of our marriage services should coordinate with that fact. Considering the emotions produced by the sight of wedding gowns and floral decorations, our attempts at attention-grabbing probably reek like skunkweeds at a rose show.

The Lord supplied us with numerous resources in Scripture. We do well to make use of them. In the early years, I used 1 Corinthians 13 frequently, and often adapted mutual vows for the couple based on that text. I usually asked them to join hands and repeat after me, "Our love will be patient and kind . . . ." It has greater impact when we use language from modern translations. The King James Version sounds romantic to some, but many young persons don't understand what it means. For that matter, many older people don't either.

By using a little imagination, we can create memorable services for special couples. When our son Rob, and daughter-in-law, Julie, asked me to officiate at their wedding, we lived in Los Angeles; Julie and her family in Dallas. At the time Rob was in the Air Force stationed at Merced, California. Marrying Rob meant that Julie had to leave her home in Texas, where she had spent all her life, and move to California, a state she had never visited.

I based the lesson on the story of Rebekah in Genesis 24. She left her family in Haran in order to marry Isaac. Rebekah traveled hundreds of miles knowing that she might never see her family again. But she went voluntarily. So did Julie.

TAILORING SERVICES TO THE COUPLE

During the scores of weddings in which I have shared, I have never witnessed any two like persons. What an exciting variety of individuals the Lord has placed around us. Time and opportunity permitting, I think it's beneficial and challenging to tailor ceremonies to the celebrants. Joyful creativity exalts and makes marriage special. It encourages people to be a part of it.

A couple, both of whom had advanced degrees in aeronautical engineering, asked me to perform their ceremony. I designed the service to fit their background. In it I quoted lines from Robert Frost's "Master Speed," and yes, the ceremony contained a biblical theme. We want to avoid triteness while still bringing some of the couple's milieu into view.

If the couple appreciates the arts, quote from or use themes from their favorite poetry, plays, etc. If they enjoy the outdoors, an endless possibility exists for references and themes. Solomon used the motif of God's creation in the springtime in Song of Songs, "Flowers appear on the earth; the season of singing has come, the cooing of doves is heard in our land. . . . Arise, come, my darling; my beautiful one, come with me" (S. of S. 2:12, 13).

THE NEED TO BE POSITIVE

Several years ago, a friend in Northern California attended a wedding service conducted by a young man whom I had met. The friend told me that after listening to the young minister warn in his sermon about all the problems to be expected, he wondered why anyone would want to get married. Cover the cautions in the counseling sessions. Celebrate the possibilities in the marriage service.

MEASURING LENGTH

It was a humid day in July when I officiated for the wedding of our daughter, Janice, and son-in-law, Lloyd. The building lacked air-conditioning. Lloyd wears glasses. He said if I had talked any longer that day, the sweltering heat would have caused his glasses to slide right off his nose. Actually, it was one of my briefer services. Neither Janice nor Lloyd has ever favored long ceremonies of any kind.

How lengthy should weddings be? "A sermon doesn't have to be eternal to be immortal," my predecessor at the Church of Christ in Hollywood used to say. Tailor the length to the type of service. Usually when people spend more they want to see a greater result. But, it's probably best that the only thing long on the day of the wedding is the bridal gown.

I base this brevity plea on several considerations. One of the foremost is sympathy for those in the bridal party. Remember the last time you stood at attention in an unfamiliar location for an extended period of time? Standing on a raised platform before a group of strangers while wearing weighty attire and bearing a sweaty glow makes clock-watchers out of the hardiest of best men and bridesmaids.

Second, we want to leave the gathered loved ones with the impression that they desire to hear more, not that they've heard too much. A short supply of any commodity increases its worth. We need to say enough to dignify the occasion. Lincoln took just a few minutes to hallow the grounds at Gettysburg. Unbelievers are often present at weddings. It's an excellent opportunity to show them that Christians practice good economics.

THE PLACE OF HUMOR

I've probably been criticized more for my use of humor than for any other factor. Some of my enemies excoriated me roundly for joking and jesting. My friends and loved ones still question my use of stories at times. These criticisms are often correct. I admit to telling stories in my sermons on occasion just to get laughs. For that I deserve censure and welcome it.

But talks lacking humor tend to become dry, didactic, and tiring. Jesus used humor. His story about the fellow who tried to avoid swallowing a gnat but gulped a camel probably brought chuckles. As long as we refrain from lewdness and don't use humor to insult, demean, or mock, it's a valuable asset. It provides pleasant breaks and puts people at ease — all except those whose shirts are stuffed too tightly.

How can we use humor? It works well as a foil for more serious points. We can take people to greater depths of reflection if we allow them to join us on short, playful jaunts. I often use humor as a bridge between the sermon (where I have addressed the need for patient love) and the vows.

Earlier I mentioned a ceremony I performed for a mature couple — she is an Armenian, and he is a Mexican-American. At the end of my remarks on never ending love, I said to the couple, "Some day, Ramon, you will come home from work, weary, exhausted, and hungry, only to find out that Hasmig has burned your favorite enchiladas. That's when you will need that enduring love. And some evening, Hasmig, when you have those enchiladas prepared to perfection, and have the table set by candlelight, Ramon will call to say that he has to work late, and he's not sure when he'll be home. That's when your love will need to be everlasting." Use what works best for you.

USING POETRY EFFECTIVELY

Short poetic sections to emphasize points or dramatize thoughts add a pleasant dimension. It helps to read books of poetry to perfect our skills. The ability to recite poetry effectively is almost a lost art. Few persons do it well. If we can improve our proficiency in reading it publicly, our listeners will probably find particular enjoyment. Most readers make the mistake of emphasizing the poetic meter and rhyme rather than the text and its meaning.

It's best to read verse as we read prose, naturally accenting the words as in ordinary conversation. This conveys the thoughts more smoothly and effectively. The minds of the hearers still perceive the rhyme as written by the author. Before I read poetry publicly, I retype or rewrite the lines as if they were prose to help me read as I have described.

SUGGESTIONS REGARDING PRAYERS

Jesus cautioned us against the use of long, repetitious prayers. The Lord doesn't hear them, and probably neither do most people at wedding services. If we trained the video cameras on the audience during prayers at weddings or any type of service, we would likely find many of the guests staring into space or nervously checking their watches.

By respecting a few principles, we can improve the effects of our prayers. First, prayers are not teaching mechanisms, but honest communications of our hearts to the Lord. Second, because many people at wedding ceremonies are novices at religion, they probably should be given smaller doses of it. Third, we pray on behalf of the couple and their families. Finally, we exalt God, His goodness, love, and wisdom. We avoid self-aggrandizement.

How then can we communicate the important aspects in prayer? It probably works better if we offer two or three brief prayers at conspicuous moments in the ceremony where we can address specific needs in short sentences. Leave long prayers for our private confessionals to the Lord.

HOMEMADE VOWS

Many couples request to write and recite their own vows. This is good. Wedding services mean more to those who help design them. A few principles are in order if the couple chooses to do this.

Be supportive, but ask to see the vows prior to rehearsal. Tactfully say that you would like to make sure that your comments relate to their vows. Getting to see the vows beforehand gives you the opportunity to review what they write. This helps avoid duplication of remarks. It also enables you to deal with any serious grammatical errors or comments that violate Christian principles. It vexed me to discover that numerous couples planned to write vows but never got them finished by wedding time because of other exigencies. Give the candidates a deadline well before the wedding for completing them.

RING CEREMONIES

Ministers say much about the perpetuity of love symbolized by the circular form of wedding rings. Bands also make public statements about belonging. In addition, our mates honor us by conferring such a gift before a crowd of witnesses. This part of the marriage service deserves some original thought and creativity.

The couple might appreciate it if you give them a choice between two or three selections or ideas. Have a few ring ceremonies copied and on hand. You may then review them with the couple so they can select their preference. I confess to using little creativity in this part of the service. I'll probably wish I had done better into perpetuity.

Suggestion: use short phrases in the vow and ring ceremonies.

The couple will have difficulty repeating after us if we give them extended or complicated phraseology.

DECLARATIONS OF MARRIAGE

By the time we get to the declaration in the actual service, we can usually sense anticipation in the wedding party and the congregation. The moment of wedded bliss beckons. But before it takes place, we must utter a declaration that's usually worded in long, complicated phrases. The statement traces the bases on which it is founded. The candidates have accepted each other, stated vows of fidelity to each other, and exchanged rings. All this is done in the presence of God and the assembled witnesses. We state the authority by which we unite them.

We are ministers of the gospel, and on that basis the state in which we perform the ceremony empowers us to officiate. That's a lot to say in a single sentence. Nothing but tradition prohibits us from breaking the statement into more manageable portions. Your tongue and lungs may appreciate it, too.

USE OF THE LORD'S SUPPER

Baptism and the Lord's table are the only true biblical rites or sacraments. Because Communion represents the oneness of God's people, forgiveness through the blood of Jesus, God's covenant relationship with us, and our hope of resurrection, we are wise to consider certain questions prior to using it in a marriage service.

Does serving the elements only to the couple agree with Jesus' command to the apostles "to drink from it, all of you"? Second, how will we deal with the issue of non-Christians present at the ceremony who don't wish to participate? Third, will the service exalt God's work in Christ?

TAPING THE SERVICE

At most services today, someone videotapes the ceremony. Usually, several persons present have their cameras operating. But the quality of sound obtained through these devices isn't always the best. And, on occasion, no one brings one. I think it's good to make an audiotape that you can present to the couple. In my opinion, they can concentrate better on its meaning as they listen later, because the visual pictures will not distract them.

PREPARING YOUR NOTES

I witnessed a ceremony many years ago led by a colleague with a photographic memory. He used no notes for any part of the ceremony. Most of us could do that, but I'm not sure the time spent memorizing names, the sermon, and the procedures would be worth it.

Some ministers carry heavy Bibles into the service loaded with copious notes. Unless a stand or pulpit is available at ring time, they have to tuck their Scriptures under their arms and hope their notes don't fall out. I prefer typing or writing the service notes on four by six cards. I always number them in the event that they should drop accidentally. Bold letters make good paragraph headings and different colors help mark transitions in the ceremony (RING CEREMONY, VOWS, etc.). That way I can easily scan them.

I started using a variety of colors after noting well into a ceremony that the father of the bride was still standing in the aisle. "What's he doing there?" I thought to myself. Then I realized I had forgotten to ask him, "Who gives the bride away?" Four by six cards can easily be placed in my inner coat pocket. If you don't have a method you are comfortable with, you can cautiously experiment.

Not long ago at a funeral service conducted by an experienced minister, he referred to the deceased's mother using the wrong name. It incensed one family member. I'm not sure the ad-libbing minister was aware of his mistake. Making incorrect references can be both embarrassing and anger provoking at funerals and weddings.

How can we avoid making this error? I write the names of the couple in my notes. If I plan to use the notes again, I pencil them in so they can be erased for the next usage.

CONGREGATIONAL PARTICIPATION

We have almost no descriptions of services of any kind from New Testament times. But worship services in the Old Testament period seem to have featured congregational participation. The writers of Psalms designed many of them to be read antiphonally. The whole nation participated in the blessing-cursing ceremony described in Deuteronomy 27:12, 13.

We do well to follow that example — not in cursing of course, but in involving the congregation. We can do this by using responsive and unison readings, congregational hymns, and the Lord's Prayer or other unison prayers. Participatory services of all kinds create interest, overcome boredom, and involve worshipers. No spouse should hear snoring until after the wedding.

Unity Candle Services

Upon completion of their vows in the service, some couples like to signify their new oneness by means of a unity candle ceremony. Individual candles representing the bride and groom are lighted prior to the ceremony. After the vows they use their individual candles to simultaneously light a single, usually larger candle which represents their indivisibility. Often they extinguish their individual candles, though some couples prefer to keep theirs lighted to signify that they want to retain their own individuality.

One caution. Don't depend on others to practice safety in the use of lighted candles. Keep candles a safe distance from flammable objects and promptly extinguish them at the end of the service. Better to marshal this part of the service than to deal with the Fire Marshal.

Printed Programs

In longer services, printed programs help the congregation follow along. Programs have the added benefit of enabling those in attendance to identify not only the participants but also the location of Scriptures and the titles of songs. Having this information printed also saves the minister from serving as an emcee.

However we and the couple might design the ceremony, Paul's advice to the Corinthians always applies, "Everything should be done in a fitting and orderly way" (1 Corinthians 14:40).

Chapter Seven

USE OF OTHER
FACILITIES AND
MATTERS OF PROTOCOL

USING OTHER FACILITIES

At times you may find yourself officiating in an unfamiliar setting. If no sexton or custodian will be present, arrive early enough to familiarize yourself with all the necessary facilities and light switches. Better yet, make sure some reliable person knows.

An attorney friend once asked me to officiate for him and his fiancée. We held the ceremony in a nearby town on the afternoon of New Year's Eve; he wanted a tax deduction for the full year. He arranged for the use of the large church building with which he and I were both unfamiliar. We rehearsed two evenings prior. All went smoothly.

Yet the day of the wedding made me wish that I had available to me a checklist utilizing the information in this manual. The church sexton was present on the night of the rehearsal but not on the wedding day. Guests began arriving, and we were beset with two problems, and two more to come.

The guests had to be seated in a dark building because none of us had a clue as to the location of the light switches. And we couldn't find the marriage license. My friend, the groom, whom I had known for years and trusted ninety-nine percent, insisted that he had brought the license on the night of the rehearsal. My one percent doubt prevailed.

As we groped for switches and sought the license, suddenly the organ sounded and the first soloist began singing. I ran through the dark, unfamiliar territory up to where the organist was seated to ask why she had begun. She referred me to the order of service the bride had given her, pointing to the instructions which read, "At 2:01 p.m. soloist will begin." Also on that list, which I had not seen, the bride had set precise times for all the other parts of the ceremony.

I requested the organist not to proceed until I instructed her. There was an embarrassingly long interval between the first soloist and the balance of the ceremony. After several more minutes, someone went to the sexton's house. Fortunately it was nearby. Not only did we obtain the location of the light switches, we also found the missing marriage license. The sexton had taken it home. Finally, we were ready to start. The processional took place in orderly fashion. It looked as though everything would work smoothly.

Both the bride and groom had performed leading roles in Southern California musical comedies. They planned to sing to each other during the wedding. He sang his on pitch without a hitch. She bawled. She couldn't finish. She remained red-eyed throughout the ceremony.

The lessons in this story are numerous. If you are in strange territory, make sure someone knows the location of the rest rooms, the telephones, and the light switches — and how to operate the sound system. Also remember to get keys to all the rooms and cabinets.

OUTSIDE SETTINGS

A few years ago a couple asked me to perform their service at one of my favorite Los Angeles locations — the top of Mount Hollywood. This is not the mountain where the Hollywood sign is located, but one a little east of there that overlooks Griffith Observatory. Mount Hollywood affords a spectacular view of a large portion of Los Angeles. You can see the downtown area on the east, Palos Verdes Peninsula on the south, and Century City and Santa Monica on the west. On a clear day even Catalina Island, twenty-six miles off shore, comes into view.

Outdoor settings make ideal locations. They usually require fewer decorations, less clean up, and God's creation provides excellent backdrops. For the Mount Hollywood wedding the couple got a permit from the park ranger. By special arrangement a ranger escorted us on a fire trail in our automobiles to the site. Rangers also permitted them to erect a temporary white picket fence. This helped define and enclose the area; the park cannot be closed to the public.

But precautions are always in order when using outdoor settings. Secure permits if needed or have someone reserve the site well in advance. Other considerations include: Will mosquitoes, ants or flies attack the participants? Will noise from nearby model airplanes or baseball games interfere? Has the couple made alternate plans in the event of inclement weather? Wind plays terrible tricks on wedding attire; have they made provision for that? In gusty areas the bride may need ballast in her hems.

Does your voice carry sufficiently to be heard in an outdoor setting? I'm not gifted with a stentorian voice. Having sufficient volume is always a problem for me. If no amplifying system is used, ask someone standing in the back of the crowd to signal to you whether your voice is being heard adequately. But choose someone who wants to hear you.

MATTERS OF PROTOCOL

When officiating at another church building — When we are asked to perform ceremonies in church buildings where the bride and groom know the minister but choose us, it calls for tactful diplomacy. I've been on both sides of the situation. Generally, the bride's minister presides. At times, though, the bride or groom may have a favorite uncle or old family friend whom they wish to have officiate.

I recommend that we follow the example of Jesus whenever we are faced with either being the chosen or rejected one. How do we practice that? If the couple does not decide to have us preside, we pray for a forgiving spirit, and wish the couple our best in the Lord.

If we become the chosen one, we treat the rejected one as we would like to be treated. First, we might ask the couple if they would like the home minister to have a part in the service. Possibly they desire for him/her to read Scripture, say a prayer, etc. If the couple prefers not to have the home minister participate, I think it's good to acknowledge the minister's work on behalf of the couple. Whatever is said should be honest, but complimentary.

Interfaith Weddings — Dealing with home minister situations requires wisdom and forgiveness. Handling interfaith circumstances takes prudence, planning, and Christlike patience. Where beliefs of the other minister are at total odds with the Spirit and the Word of the Lord, we may need to offer our regrets respectfully and request that the couple find another minister.

We need to assess and review our intentions carefully to avoid making decisions motivated by bitterness or pride. We win far more souls by displaying a servant spirit than with doctrinal certitude.

A gift for the couple? — My wife and I did considerable soul-searching over the question of the propriety of giving gifts. At times we not only purchased a gift, my wife also hosted the wedding shower.

Frequently for us, the issue became a money-searching situation, too. There may be times when you wish to give a gift because you are especially close to the family. However, it isn't usually expected. Also, it's probably financially impossible unless you are independently wealthy. Whatever course of action you (and your spouse) may decide in respect to gifts, remember that you will be setting a precedent that you will be expected to follow in future situations. And the needs of your family always come first.

Who should accompany the bride down the aisle? — The solo role of the father in giving the bride away is among the changing traditions over the past few decades. Attribute this to several factors. At times no father is in the picture. Some brides prefer that both of their parents accompany them. A few brides have been away from home so long that they don't feel the need to have anyone give them away. In some cases, the bride may feel closer to her stepfather than to her biological father.

No biblical precedent requires anyone to accompany the bride down the aisle. She may choose, if she wishes, to have both parents accompany her, or to walk with her father on one side and her stepfather on the other. She may also choose to walk alone.

Public displays of respect, sensitivity to the feelings of others, and gratitude, are far more important than strict formality and tradition. In fact, Jesus never gave much credence to tradition. (See Matthew 15:1-9.)

Chapter Eight

AVOIDING
REHEARSAL DEBACLE

We seek accord in wedding ceremonies. But marriage services don't always create an amalgamation of families and friends. The opposite often occurs. Most persons arrive for the services wanting joyful agreement. Some assemble warily. A few come equipped with low flash points and defective fuses. Ministers must meld this diverse gathering into a congenial group.

It's the rehearsal that's most likely to launch hull-ripping torpedoes into the love boat. Well-meaning relatives come determined to get their way. They have definite ideas about matters of procedure and who should stand where. Many don intimidating visages. Expert in destroying ministerial confidence, they express their opinions like NFL linebackers. A few are burly enough to back their views.

How do we deal with the intimated disapproval and the blatant criticism? We must ward off these visage and verbal assaults and also remember scores of details necessary for effective rehearsals. Adding to our potential woes may be the fact that the couple has hired a wedding consultant whose ideas we might not share. Who takes charge at rehearsal? Whose will prevails? Peaceful, effectual services depend on the resolution of these issues.

WHO IS IN CHARGE

If I'm not officiating in my own church building, it pleases me when the couple hires a bridal consultant because it limits my responsibilities. Some larger churches have wedding consultants on their staffs. The hired professional makes sure all in the wedding party arrive, start on cue, and take their places. It frees me to attend to the rites of which I need to take charge. I encountered few difficulties with wedding professionals. If you fear there may be a problem, clarify and resolve it immediately with the couple. Most troubles come from family members with good intentions, but highly vocalized preferences. Review all parts of the service with the couple prior to rehearsal. Follow the bride's wishes. It's her wedding. You are in charge of the service, however. Communicate that pleasantly but firmly. Your self-assured, good-natured expression of this will cause most interfering persons to back off.

You may have to say something like, "Lucy, Tim and I already discussed this. This is Lucy's wedding, and this is the way we're going to do it. Loving Lucy and Tim as you do, I know that you want to respect their wishes." If you don't display confidence and act resolutely, you are in for a long, frustrating rehearsal that makes no one happy. Leave nothing to chance or with the hope that you will resolve that detail later. Murphy's Law operates exponentially at weddings.

POSITIONING AND PROCESSIONALS

Numerous factors dictate positioning of the various participants in a wedding ceremony. The bride often prefers to have her attendants stand in proximity representing her feelings toward them. Her closest friend is her maid of honor, her next best friend is the first attendant, etc.

Other brides worry about height gradations. If they are short, they prefer that the taller ones stand away from them. At times, compatibility of the attendant and her usher/escort becomes a factor. I usually let the couple deal with these concerns. Such things as building configurations, size of the platform, and altar area also become items to consider. Only so many "actors" can get on stage comfortably.

In formal weddings, ushers usually accompany the bridal attendants down the aisle. Some prefer to have the men and women enter separately. As long as the couple's wishes are in good taste and are biblical, I choose not to interfere.

I do express my preference concerning whether the minister or the bridal party faces the congregation. I don't feel comfortable standing with my back to an audience. My moderate voice is barely audible. But the congregation should not have to look at the backs of the bridal party seeing only my creased countenance. I prefer to face the audience and have the bridal couple face each other. What marvelous memories I have of watching emotions in the faces of couples as they look into each other's eyes while reciting their vows. With this positioning, the congregation sees the couple, too.

TWENTY-TWO REHEARSAL HINTS

The following points are crucial to a smooth, efficient rehearsal:

1. Before the rehearsal, the bride and groom should give you a list of the attendants and what place they are assigned in the processional. Prepare the order of service. At the rehearsal give copies to all who might be assisting and performing, e.g., organist and soloist. (Review with the couple prior to the rehearsal: who will spread the aisle runner if one is used, and at what point in the ceremony; and who will unroll the pew ribbons in the event they are used for the service.)

2. Line up the participants in the back of the building and have them stand in the order that they will follow at the service. This includes candle lighters, bride, bride's maids, maid of honor, flower girl, ring bearer, parents, grandparents, and the ushers assigned to seat them.

3. Remind all participants of the basic rule — *they face the bride at all times during the ceremony.*

4. Instruct the ushers.

❖ I usually found that I could review assignments with the ushers while awaiting the arrival of latecomers to the rehearsal. It isn't necessary to have all the ushers present for this. Ask one of those already present to instruct the others. Most of them gladly accept the responsibility and carry it out efficiently. This also makes better use of your time.

❖ Before the rehearsal, the couple should also designate which ushers they prefer to have seat the parents, grand-parents, etc. Review the assignments with the ushers. Demonstrate how to offer their arms to the mother or grandmother and to ask their male escorts to follow them to their designated seats.

❖ Inform the ushers on the location of rest rooms, drinking fountains, telephones, fire extinguishers, and light switches.

Because you will be busy with the ceremony, impress on the ushers that they must take charge in the event of an emergency. It's their place to call paramedics or police. They need access to the telephone and must have emergency numbers at hand.

5. Review the assignments of those performing special tasks.

Will someone be giving a special reading or will the soloist use the lectern? The reader should know beforehand whether he/she will carry the reading to the lectern or have it in place beforehand. Will they have to turn on lectern lights or adjust the microphone? Have these items clearly understood.

6. Advise the bride to bring dummies to the rehearsal.

Dummies? Most brides carry bouquets during their wed-ding services and must pass the bouquets to their bridesmaids for the vow and ring ceremonies. The bridesmaids, in turn, pass their bouquets to the next attendant so they can hold the bride's bouquets and assist with the rings. Therefore, the per-sons involved should bring dummy bouquets to rehearsal. Clutches of gift-ribbon bows from bridal showers work well for this.

7. Review cues with the bride's mother.

It's customary at wedding ceremonies for the bride's mother to lead the congregation in standing when the bride appears at the rear of the church building to make her entrance, to be seated when the wedding party is all in place, and to stand or sit at other appropriate moments in the service. Inform her and review with her the arranged cues for doing this. Some clergypersons like to say "All rise!" in a commanding voice. I prefer to nod and allow the mother to lead. It has always proved adequate.

8. In the order established, light the candles, seat the grandparents and parents, have the soloist sing, etc., so everyone gets accustomed to coming in at his/her place.

The following seating order is customary:

❖ Friends of the bride and her family are seated on the left side of the building as they enter. Friends of the groom and his family sit on the right. If an imbalance develops, ushers should begin asking guests whether they would mind sitting on the opposite side.

❖ Once the guests are seated, first the paternal, then the maternal grandparents are ushered to their seats. It's the best man's duty to determine whether the grandparents need a place to sit while they are waiting to be escorted.

❖ An usher escorts the groom's mother to her seat; usually the first or second pew on the right, one seat from the aisle. The father follows her and the usher. If they are divorced, she usually sits alone or with her present husband. The groom's father sits behind them alone, or with his present wife.

❖ Finally, the bride's mother is ushered to her seat in the left front, leaving one space on the aisle for the bride's father to sit once he gives the bride away.

❖ In the event of divorce, she sits alone or with her present husband. The bride's father would then sit immediately behind the mother either alone or with his new wife.

❖ In instances where there is a divorce but no remarriage by either, I've seen father and mother sit together out of deference to family unity.

❖ If both mother and father escort the bride down the aisle, the ushers need instructions on how to reserve the appropriate seating for them.

9. Discuss with the ushers how they can deal with late-comers and parents with crying babies.

Come to agreement on these matters with the bride and groom beforehand. Persons of various cultures tend to see the importance of these things differently. In any case, guests who arrive late shouldn't be seated during the processional, and should be seated afterward only if it can be done without interrupting the ceremony. Babies have no place at weddings or funerals, in my opinion, and should never be permitted to disrupt any worship service. Instruct ushers to deal tactfully but firmly with these matters.

10. If the bride and groom have not hired a bridal counselor, ask them to appoint someone to oversee the processional.

Give this person a copy of the order of service. Have him/her start the participants down the aisle on the proper cues reminding them to walk at the right pace.

11. Walk the bridal party through the entire service establishing the pace, spacing, and positioning on the platform or altar area.

Be mindful that wedding gowns require more space than the garb usually worn at rehearsals. Also, when bridal attendants make their turns on the platform, they should turn so that they always face the bride. Will the bride's gown have a long train? Make sure that the bride has appointed someone to assist her with it.

12. Should you use a stand-in for the bride at rehearsal?

This practice is based on an old superstition that the bride's participation brings bad luck to the marriage. We do well to discourage belief in superstitions. Having the bride present helps build her confidence for the day of the wedding.

13. Practice everything but the homily and the vows.

If the couple will be reciting their own vows, it's wise to have them rehearse these, too.

Will the bride's father be presenting her (giving her away)? Review with him at what point in the aisle he releases his daughter to the groom. He should be on the bride's left and escort her to where the groom stands awaiting her. The groom waits at her right and offers his left arm.

The point of transfer depends on building configuration, and/or denominational requirements. Usually the transfer takes place near the front pew. The father remains there until the minister asks, "Who gives Lucy to be married to Tim?" After he has presented his daughter, he steps to his designated place and takes his seat. Either then or before — this is up to you — the groom and bride proceed to the platform or altar area.

In the event the bride has more than one escort, e.g., father and mother, or father and stepfather, they can stand on either side of the bride and release her one step before she reaches the groom.

14. Review with the maid of honor and best man the manner in which they will retain the rings until they give them to you for the ring ceremony.

I don't recommend putting them on the ring bearer's pillow. Many things can go wrong. I've seen the little guys so overcome by stage fright that they never make it to the front. Many times they don't stay; they run off to their mothers never to be seen again. In the few cases when the ring bearers perform as they should, often either the best man or maid of honor has trouble untying those dainty ribbons or fumbles the ring.

In my opinion, it's better if the best man keeps the ring in a small pocket of his vest or jacket, and for the maid of honor to wear the groom's ring on her little finger a little past the first joint. Practice, also, the transferring of bouquets for the vow and ring ceremonies.

15. Practice holding and reading your notes, Bible, or manual.

I've discovered that in inadequate lighting my eyes often fail me. Also, floor mikes present a problem for me when I try to hold my notes in front of me.

16. Be especially sensitive to the feelings of parents and grandparents.

Honestly compliment them during the service for rearing the bride and groom.

17. Do your best to learn the names of the bridal party.

18. What if your daughter asks you to give her away and also to officiate at her wedding?

Possibilities include:

❖ Have a solo or musical number at the time of transfer. Your daughter and the groom can remain in place, and you can proceed to the altar during the music.

❖ Ask a minister friend to preside until that point in the service. A seat either on the platform or the front pew can be reserved for this person to sit in once you come to the platform.

19. The recessional order is usually the reverse of the processional.

When the bride and groom kiss, it usually signals the end of the ceremony. It's time for the recessional. Some ministers announce the couple by saying, "I'd like to introduce Tim and Lucy Linn," or, "I'd like to present Mr. and Mrs. Linn."

It's a nice touch to have the bride and groom pause on their way to the rear of the building to greet, hug, and thank their parents and grandparents.

After the bride and groom leave the platform, the best man offers his right arm to the maid (or matron) of honor, and they leave together. Then the first groomsman offers his arm to the first bridal attendant, and they leave the platform together. Then the second groomsman offers his arm to the second bridal attendant, etc.

If a flower girl and ring bearer take part in the ceremony, the bride and groom may choose to have the little ones follow them off the platform. The children may also follow the best man and maid of honor, or they may be last off the platform.

20. Remember the parents and grandparents.

Once the bridal party is off the platform, the ushers return to escort the parents and grandparents in the reverse order that they were seated.

21. Does the receiving line form in the back of the building or at some other location?

At times, the couple chooses to have a receiving line at the church building. In that event, all in the bridal party should immediately take their places in line to greet the guests.

22. When does the minister leave the service?

I usually remain in my place in order to make sure that all in the party leave the platform appropriately and to give any needed instructions to the guests. Guests should stay in their seats until the parents and grandparents are escorted out, and/or until the ushers can dismiss them row by row.

FINAL NOTE: Find something positive to say about every person in the wedding party. Make the occasion fun.

Chapter Nine

TWELVE TIPS

FOR THE DAY OF THE SERVICE, AND TEN ASSORTED EXTRAS

TWELVE TIPS

Your follow-up on a few essentials will make the difference between happiness and grief for you and all concerned on the day of the wedding.

1. Double-check your notes.

Check that you have them. Once at a wedding service where I co-officiated, the ceremony proceeded smoothly until the bride and groom stood before us. Suddenly, the other minister turned brilliant red with embarrassment. Then he explained that he had forgotten his notes, and hastened off the platform to locate them. Fortunately, we were in his church building.

Check that your data are in order. At a funeral my wife and I attended recently, the presiding minister forgot to bring his obituary notes. The tension created by forgetting them or having them out of order for an important event probably brings the moment of our own funerals a day or two closer.

2. Double-check your grooming.

Better yet have someone else give you an honest inspection. Unruly hair, unzipped trousers, or a few square inches of toilet paper can mar an otherwise sound ceremony.

217

3. Pray with the bride and groom prior to the ceremony.

We need the Lord's wisdom, guidance and strength. Praying helps us focus. It reassures the bride and groom. Let them know during the counseling sessions of your plans to pray. Because the bride and groom usually wait in different parts of the building and don't see each other prior to the ceremony, separate prayers may be necessary. It's probably best for the bride if we wait until she is fully dressed for the ceremony.

In some localities, there is a custom called "Presenting or Presented to the Groom." After the bride is dressed for the service, she is escorted to a room where she and the groom spend time admiring each other and conversing privately. Later the photographer is called to take shots of the couple. Some favor this custom as it shortens the time afterward for picture taking. If the couple follows this custom, it would make a convenient time for prayer.

4. Have the license in hand prior to the ceremony.

In fact, get it before rehearsal. One inexperienced minister I know performed a ceremony for a couple who had no license. He didn't find this out until afterward. Fortunately the authorities dealt with him compassionately.

5. Make sure the best man does his job.

His task is to ensure that everyone is accommodated and comfortable. Clarify his duties with the couple before the rehearsal, review them with him at the rehearsal, and follow-up with him the day of the wedding.

6. Reassure all participants.

In the last half-hour before the wedding march, participants perspire and display various signs of nervousness. Ask them if they have questions or if there are things about the ceremony that they don't understand. Review their duties with them patiently to help them with any uncertainties. Compliment them. Begin your praise on rehearsal night to build their confidence.

Let them know the correct things they have done. Then they will have fewer apprehensions about the matters that need improvement. Be sure to tell both male and female attendants how nice they look. Ease tension by using brief comments, e.g., "We've never lost anyone yet at a wedding," and, "The little miscues we make today, we'll probably laugh at in a month or two."

We say these things to those who seem overly concerned about making mistakes. On rare occasions, we come across flippant persons. These need the opposite approach but always in private.

7. Deal with photographers.

Most professional photographers ask permission before shooting in a church building, but not all. And many amateurs don't know that they should ask. Review your policy with the couple early enough to inform their photographer. Ask the ushers to enforce the policy.

While attending the wedding of a neighbor, Norma and I were amazed to see the bride's mother stand up with a movie camera as the bride came down the aisle. The camera was equipped with a huge bank of bright lights, which she kept trained on her daughter through most of the ceremony. It seemed to us, that she was attempting to preserve a memory she never got to enjoy in the first place.

At times it's a moot question whether the minister, the mother of the bride, or the bridal counselor is in charge of weddings. Actually, photographers rule many of them. They often spend more time creating wedding scenes afterward than the ceremony took in the first place. You will have to deal with this problem based on your own time constraints and church building calendar. I favor the current trend of taking pictures before the service.

8. How to deal with reluctant grooms and no-show brides.

Most grooms eagerly go through the door into the wedding chapel. They just want to get the ceremony over. But now and then you will discover a reluctant groom. Anxiety sets in just before the prelude music. Mild reticence can be overcome with a little humorous coaxing.

If you discover serious doubts surfacing, you may want to delay the start for whatever length of time it takes to resolve them. Proper premarital counseling usually circumvents this problem.

What if the bride doesn't show? Norma and I stood waiting at the church building with a groom and several guests for a bride who never arrived. The couple had known each other for years and had dated a considerable length of time. She was a few decades younger than he, and we suspect, became uncomfortable with the age difference. The rejection hurt him deeply. The failure was partly mine; I didn't give adequate counseling.

If you cancel on the day of the wedding, however, you face an immediate problem. What do you tell the guests? First, you need to determine that the bride was not involved in a car accident or locked inadvertently in the bathroom. Once you ascertain her reluctance, you can ask the best man to announce that there will be no wedding. He should do this in a brief factual statement that doesn't attempt to place blame on anyone.

Norma and I learned another hard-earned lesson. We purchased a silver bowl for the groom and his no-show bride. On it we had engraved their names and the "wedding date." We kept it in the closet for years as a memento of our bad judgment. We finally sold it at a garage sale very cheap.

9. Select a strong, understanding person to oversee child participants.

W.C. Fields insisted that he didn't like to share the stage with children and animals. He may have made bad choices concerning his liver, but he spoke wisely of the risk of being upstaged by children. When a child does unpredictable things in a ceremony, it often amuses doting parents and grandparents, but it usually tests, dismays, and frustrates everyone else involved. It also detracts attention from the bride.

Review the potentialities of the situation early with the prospective bride and groom. If they insist upon using a recalcitrant child in the ceremony, ask them to appoint a capable adult that can quickly and unobtrusively lead the little one off the platform and into the wings if it becomes necessary.

At a recent wedding, the bride used a novel approach to coax the toddler flower girls. She placed bride dolls at the steps of the altar and told the little girls that they could walk to the front, get their dolls, and then go back and sit with their parents. It worked beautifully.

10. If you should have to deal with the press.

On rare occasions, we may be asked to unite couples of public note. Reporters might crowd near the church entrance and call late at night seeking interviews or wedding details. We should give no information unless we obtain full approval from the parties involved.

Reporters may be there for another reason. Misfortunes and tragedies occur without warning and under many circumstances. We do well to react taciturnly to news photographers and journalists until we can speak advisedly and factually.

11. Verify that the best man and maid of honor have the rings in readiness.

12. Complete the license and have it signed immediately after the ceremony.

Photocopy the license for your files and mail it at the first opportunity.

Some states provide a wedding certificate for the bride and groom. It's not a legal document, only an unofficial record of the ceremony. After filling it out, hand it to the best man. He can give it to the groom later.

Some prefer to have the license signed during the ceremony as part of the service. If this is done, make it a priority to retrieve it as soon as possible after the service, especially if the wedding isn't held in your church building.

NOTE: As the officiant, it is your responsibility to complete and mail the license. In many states this must be done within forty-eight hours of the ceremony. Most states have penalties for failure to comply with the above.

TEN ASSORTED EXTRAS

Every service brings the possibility of surprises and interruptions. If we know how to deal with them in advance, the greater the chance that these interruptions will be brief and insignificant. What sorts of things can go wrong?

1. A former suitor of the bride or friend of the groom may try to interfere.

This happens not only in the movies. Because it's been depicted so often in the cinema, it's likelier to occur in real situations. So what can we do?

First, we circumvent it by reducing the opportunities for it to take place. I don't use the comment, "If any man can show just cause why they may not be lawfully joined together . . ." Fully research this information in the counseling sessions. It makes public questions and comments unnecessary. Second, include in your instructions to the ushers plans for dealing with intrusions.

2. Lost rings.

Once I waited at least an hour for the bride and groom to show up at an informal wedding. Several guests waited with me. When the couple finally arrived, the bride was in tears. They had forgotten to purchase rings until the last minute. Then they couldn't find a jewelry store open. Someone in the wedding party made a temporary loan of a personal ring to use for the ceremony.

3. No-shows among the attendants.

Car trouble, lost keys, and bad directions conspire to create latecomers for all occasions. If you face one of these difficulties, consult with the bride, groom, and best man. Options include brief delay of the ceremony, using a stand-in attendant, or elimination of the position. Be sure to inform all the participants of the decisions that you reach. We best avoid this problem by requesting that those in the wedding party be at the site an hour or so before the ceremony.

4. Fainting.

At times, tension, tight atmosphere, and tight clothes induce fainting. Then emotions get taut. No one ever collapsed during a ceremony I conducted, but I have been present at weddings where it has happened. The minister, in one instance, simply proceeded while others tended the fallen comrade. Those of us in attendance wondered about the seriousness of the problem and had trouble keeping our attention on the service.

Fainting isn't the only reason people collapse. Once you ascertain, however, that the problem isn't serious, reassure the audience and the wedding party. State that it appears the person's problem isn't dangerous, but that you need to pause briefly to make sure. The ushers should have already been in action appropriate to the situation. You can tell people that they are free to visit in their seats. Ask the organist to play background music until the person can be revived or removed.

Extended periods of silence in circumstances of the unknown make people nervous. Unless the delay is brief, you might allow those in the wedding party to sit down until you can resume the service.

5. Intoxicated persons.

The directions you give the ushers should include instructions for dealing with those under the influence. Much of the approach depends on whether the extent of inebriation might cause disorderly, rude behavior. Otherwise it's probably best not to try to fix it.

6. Slips of the tongue.

In one of my early wedding services, I inadvertently said, "What God has joined asunder . . . ." It embarrassed me. The church building was packed with guests, and because I had sided with the bride and groom in a controversy involving the bride's sister, the bride's family didn't exactly adore me. That incident taught me to rehearse the lines and to follow my notes more carefully.

What did the couple think? We had been very close to them. At the time, he was serving a medical residency in a local hospital. After they moved out of the area, they returned annually to attend services at the church in Hollywood to celebrate what "God had joined asunder."

Unless you have extraordinarily quick wit, it's probably best to correct your verbal errors immediately without comment and proceed with the service. My impromptu attempts to correct improprieties often result in malapropisms.

7. The use of nonreligious music.

Most weddings contain nonreligious music of some type. The traditional "Wedding March" isn't a religious song. The consciences of some that I know would be offended even by its use in a religious service. A few ministers make separations. These people practice a curious casuistry. They don't regard wedding ceremonies as religious services even though they read Scriptures at them and say prayers.

In my opinion, all of life is worship. We never leave God's presence even though we design and engage at times in services that praise him in all aspects. It doesn't bother me to use what we call nonreligious music in a wedding ceremony unless the lyrics contain thoughts and phrases that one would not want to use in the Lord's presence. Those should be inappropriate in any context.

8. Should we attend rehearsal dinners and receptions?

Consider this question first: Were you invited? Don't necessarily presume your attendance is requested. Second, we must be careful stewards of our time. If we are close to the families involved, we may need to be present. But our spouse, children, or work may need our presence more.

9. Prayers at receptions.

Many people assume that ministers offer better prayers and lend dignity to events. This means that we receive invitations to lead invocations and benedictions. Only we can judge whether such participation is needful. If we refuse, we should do it with utmost politeness and respect. If we accept, we shouldn't see it as an opportunity for display or to preach. We pray with thanksgiving. We ask God to bless not only the food, but also the people present. Terse prayers are best.

10. Dealing with behavior at the wedding reception that may violate your conscience, e.g., drunkenness.

My reply, "It depends on who is doing it," may seem as though I play favorites. In fact, it is biblical to be selective in making such judgments. How so?

The principles we discover in 1 Corinthians 5 apply here. If the drunken person is non-Christian, render judgment cautiously. If the person is a Christian, use New Testament precedents to deal with it. But we always act with gentle sensitivity and tact. (See Galatians 6:1-5.)

Chapter Ten

RENEWAL OF VOWS

Couples choose to renew their vows for many reasons. In some cases, due to limited finances the wedding service was a quick, informal affair. Later the couple decides to have a renewal service of the size they wished their wedding had been.

Other couples simply desire to publicly reaffirm their love for each other. They plan these renewals so that their children, old friends, and new friends can share in the ceremony.

The renewals in which I participated were joyful ceremonies. They inhered less tension for all concerned than typical wedding services. They carry with them the opportunity to call all in attendance to reaffirm their own marriage vows. Usually little counseling is necessary. Because the couple is already married, state requirements are not a concern.

Two sample ceremonies are included. You are free to adapt or copy them. The second one includes an additional reason why some couples prefer to restate their vows.

SAMPLE RENEWAL ONE (John and Mary Smith)

Thirty-five years ago, a young couple eloped and had their marriage vows solemnized by a justice of the peace. They have lived lovingly and harmoniously, rearing several fine children in the intervening years.

225

The one thing they felt their marriage lacked was a church wedding. They always intended to have a minister lead them in their wedding vows, but the time and circumstances were never right.

Today, in the thirty-fifth year of their marriage, they have planned the fulfillment of their long awaited desire. They would like you to share this significant moment with them. They are faithful members of the Church. As fellow members in God's family, we want to participate with them as they restate and reaffirm their wedding vows.

We ask John and Mary Smith to come forward, accompanied by their children and their families.

The biblical primacy and sanctity of marriage have been exemplified in your three and half decades of life together. This is evident in your life, your demeanor, and in your determination to serve God. The Bible's design for marriage has often been obscured and forgotten in our society. That we might all renew and reaffirm the intent and design of marriage before God, we want to recite together words from Ephesians chapter five. We shall read aloud the "all" sections together. Mary will lead the women in those sections marked for women, and John will do the same with the men.

Ephesians 5:21-33 (Today's English Version)

(All) "[21]Submit yourselves to one another because of your reverence for Christ."

(Women) "[22]Wives, submit yourselves to your husbands as to the Lord. [23]For a husband has authority over his wife just as Christ has authority over the church; and Christ is himself the Savior of the church, his body. [24]And so wives must submit themselves completely to their husbands, just as the church submits itself to Christ."

(Men) "[25]Husbands, love your wives just as Christ loved the church and gave his life for it. [26]He did this to dedicate the church to God by his word, after making it clean by washing it in water, [27]in order to present the church to himself in all its beauty — pure and faultless, without spot or wrinkle or any other imperfection."

(Women) "²⁸Men ought to love their wives just as they love their own bodies. A man who loves his wife loves himself."

(Men) "²⁹(No one ever hates his own body. Instead, he feeds it and takes care of it, just as Christ does the church;"

(All) "³⁰for we are members of his body.) ³¹As the scripture says, 'For this reason a man will leave his father and mother and unite with his wife, and the two will become one.' There is a deep secret truth revealed in this scripture, which I understand as applying to Christ and the church. ³³But it also applies to you: every husband must love his wife as himself, and every wife must respect her husband."

John and Mary don't look into the future now with the same starry-eyed anticipation they did thirty-five years ago. That doesn't mean that hope is gone. Actually, they can better affirm hope in God through their experiences of His care and presence with them over the years.

They have more confident assurance than ever of a future guided and controlled by the Lord. Today, they pledge themselves anew to their belief in God's mercy and grace in their lives as they live as husband and wife.

John, will you continue to have Mary as your partner in marriage, conforming to the counsel of God's Word? Will you abide in your love for her, comforting her and honoring her regardless of physical circumstances? Will you be faithful to her as long as you both live?

Mary, will you continue to have John as your partner in marriage in accordance with God's will? Will your love for him be constant as you comfort, honor and submit to him? And will you be faithful to him as long as you both live?

Join Right Hands

I, John, reaffirm that Mary will be my wedded wife, to whom my love is pledged in fidelity, in good times and bad times, in sickness and health, in all circumstances, from today on, as long as God grants us life.

I, Mary, reaffirm that John will be my wedded husband, to whom my love is pledged in fidelity, in good times and bad, in sickness and health, in all circumstances, today onward, as God grants us life.

Inasmuch as John and Mary have reaffirmed their commitment to their marriage vows before us in God's presence, and have stated their desire to lovingly abide in those vows, we today entreat God's richest blessings on their marriage, their family, and their loved ones, the church, and all who devote themselves to the Lord.

Prayer

Kiss

(The actual names and times in the above sample have been changed. The wife died about five years after this service. A few years later, the husband remarried and moved to another state.)

SAMPLE RENEWAL TWO (Pat and Judy Whisnant)

(When this couple first met, he had never been married; she had a young son named Sean from a previous marriage.)

Order of Service

(Soloist)

(Sean ushered his grandmother to her designated seat.)
(Bridal party entered.)

Twelve years ago, Pat Whisnant and Judy Jackson fell in love and got married in a simple ceremony in Mississippi. They loved each other exceedingly. That love has not waned. But it has changed. Something special has happened making it urgent to them that they restate their vows.

Their marriage is like an exceptionally well-designed and well-decorated house — a house in which there was much joy and sharing. Yet, the house had a defect in its foundation. It lacked the element vital to total togetherness and joy.

What was missing? When Pat and Judy were married twelve years ago, Pat was not a Christian. He loved Judy. He loved Sean as he would love Drew after he was born. But Pat's conception of love would be radically altered by God's active love in his own life.

As the prophet Jeremiah observed concerning Israel, God plans great things for all of us: " 'I know the plans I have for you,' declares the LORD, 'plans to prosper you and not to harm you, plans to give you hope and a future. Then you will call upon me and come and pray to me, and I will listen to you. You will seek me and find me when you seek me with all your heart' " (Jeremiah 29:11-13).

Pat explains that he had been looking for hope and joy in his life but in all the wrong places. What a wondrous change God brought about.

Now, with that godly foundation in their lives, Pat and Judy want to renew their vows of love and commitment. They noted not long ago that it is difficult to see perfection, but love perfected over time creates a perfection of its own. They are thankful to have the Lord call them together to his completeness. In Christ, that foundation remains secure.

What is the precedent for restating or renewing vows? In Deuteronomy 29 and 30, Moses assembled Israel in Moab prior to their entrance into the Promised Land. He reminded them of the original covenant God made with them. There, they renewed their covenant with him.

(We recited here the agenda for married couples in Ephesians five, and then Pat sang a song written by him that was dedicated to Judy.)

Pat, will you continue to have Judy as your partner in marriage, submitting yourself to the counsel of God's word? Will you continue in your love for her, honoring her regardless of physical circumstances? And will you be faithful in body and mind as long as you both live?

(Repeated for Judy)

Please join your right hands, and Pat, will you repeat after me?

I, Pat, reaffirm that Judy will be my wife, to whom my love is pledged in all faithfulness, in good times and bad times, in sickness and in health, in all circumstances from today on, as long as God grants us life.

(Restated for Judy, that Pat will be her husband.)

(Soloist)

(Vows — The couple recited vows to each other that they composed.)

(Duet)

(Ring Ceremony)

Traditionally, in a ring ceremony, the bride and groom exchange rings. Pat and Judy are so proud of Sean and Drew that they also want to give them rings to symbolize their family commitment and love.

(Prayer)

(Song — "O Perfect Love")

(Declaration)

"I will betroth you to me forever; I will betroth you to me in righteousness and justice, in love and compassion. I will betroth you in faithfulness, and you will acknowledge the LORD" (Hosea 2:19, 20).

(Kiss)

(Bridal party leaves the platform.)

Chapter Eleven

SAMPLE
WEDDING SERVICES

Included for your convenience is the traditional ceremony taken from the *Book of Common Prayer*. This service has been used for centuries.

Dearly beloved, we are gathered together here in the sight of God, and in the face of this company, to join together this man and this woman in holy matrimony; which is an honorable estate, instituted of God, signifying unto us the mystical union that is betwixt Christ and His church: which holy estate Christ adorned and beautified with His presence and first miracle that He wrought in Cana of Galilee, and is commended of Saint Paul to be honorable among all men: and therefore is not to be entered into unadvisedly or lightly; but reverently, discreetly, advisedly, soberly, and in the fear of God. Into this holy estate these two persons present now come to be joined. If any man can show just cause why they may not lawfully be joined together, let him now speak, or else hereafter forever hold his peace.

(The minister says to the candidate.)

I require and charge you both, as ye will answer at the dreadful day of judgment when the secrets of all hearts shall be disclosed, that if either of you know any impediment, why ye may not be lawfully joined together in matrimony, ye do now confess it. For be ye well assured, that if any persons are joined together otherwise than as God's Word doth allow, their marriage is not lawful.

_____ Name in full _____ , wilt thou have this woman to thy wedded wife, to live together after God's ordinance in the holy estate of matrimony? Wilt thou love her, comfort her, honor and keep her in sickness and in health; and forsaking all others, keep thee only unto her, so long as ye both live?
(The groom answers, "I will.")

_____ Name in full _____ , wilt thou have this man to thy wedded husband, to live together after God's ordinance in the holy estate of matrimony? Wilt thou love him, comfort him, honor and keep him in sickness and in health; and forsaking all others, keep thee only unto him, as long as you both live?
(The bride answers, "I will.")

Who giveth this woman to be married to this man?
(After the father's response, the minister asks bride and groom to join right hands and repeat after him as follows:)

I _____ (husband's full name) _____ , take thee _____ (bride's full name) _____ , to my wedded wife, to have and to hold from this day forward; for better for worse, for richer for poorer, in sickness and in health, to love and to cherish, till death do us part, according to God's holy ordinance; and thereto I plight thee my troth.
(They rejoin right hands.)

I _____ (woman's full name) _____ , take thee _____ (man's full name) _____ , to my wedded husband, to have and to hold from this day forward; for better for worse, for richer for poorer, in sickness and in health, to love and to cherish, till death do us part, according to God's holy ordinance; and thereto I plight thee my troth.

(Here, the minister asks for the ring, hands it to the groom instructing him to put it on the third finger of the woman's left hand, and then to repeat after him.)

With this ring I thee wed: in the name of the Father, and of the Son and of the Holy Spirit. (If it is a double ring ceremony, repeat with the bride.)

(Optional — before giving the ring to the groom for him to put on the bride's finger, the minister may bless the ring as follows.)

Bless, O Lord, this ring, that he who gives it and she who wears it may abide in Thy peace, and continue in Thy favor, unto their life's end; through Jesus Christ our Lord. Amen.

(The minister then leads the couple and the congregation in the Lord's prayer followed by the prayer below.)

O Eternal God, Creator and Preserver of all mankind, Giver of all spiritual grace, the Author of everlasting life; send Thy blessing upon these Thy servants, this man and this woman, whom we bless in Thy name; that they, living faithfully together, may surely perform and keep the vow and covenant betwixt them made (whereof this ring given and received is a token and pledge), and may ever remain in Thy perfect love and peace together, and live according to Thy laws; through Jesus Christ our Lord. Amen.

(The minister may add one or both of the following prayers.)

O Almighty God, Creator of mankind, who only art the wellspring of life; bestow upon these Thy servants, if it be Thy will, the gift and heritage of children; and grant that they may see their children brought up in Thy faith and fear, to the honor and glory of Thy name; through Jesus Christ our Lord. Amen.

O God, who hast so consecrated the state of matrimony that in it is represented the spiritual marriage and unity betwixt Christ and His church; look mercifully upon these Thy servants, that they may love, honor and cherish each other, and so live together in faithfulness and patience, in wisdom and true godliness, that their home may be a haven of blessing and peace; through the same Jesus Christ our Lord, Who liveth and reigneth with Thee and the Holy Spirit ever, one God, world without end. Amen.

(Then the minister shall join their right hands together and say this.)

Those whom God hath joined together let no man put asunder.

(Declaration of marriage.)

Forasmuch as _____(name)_____ , and _____(name)_____ have consented together in holy wedlock, and have witnessed the same before God in this company, and thereto have given and pledged their troth, each to the other, and have declared the same by giving and receiving a ring and joining hands; I pronounce that they are husband and wife. In the name of the Father and of the Son, and of the Holy Spirit. Amen.

(As the husband and wife kneel, the minister adds this blessing.)

God the Father, God the Son, God the Holy Spirit, bless, preserve, and keep you; the Lord mercifully with His favor look upon you, and fill you with all spiritual benediction and grace; that you may so live together in this life, that in the world to come you may have life everlasting. Amen.

SAMPLE TAILORED CEREMONY #1

(This ceremony was written for a couple from different cultures. He was a Jewish convert to Christianity, and she a convert to Christianity who had moved to the United States from Singapore. During the ceremony, he spent several minutes commenting on the meaning of Jesus to his life and to their marriage. He effectively used illustrations that were sometimes tear evoking and frequently humorous. Because of the personal nature of his remarks, only my part of the service is included. After my earlier comments about the need for humor in services, you will probably note the absence of it in this ceremony. This was at Leo's request. I think he wanted me to play the straight man for his own humor.

Text: Psalm 107 (RSV)

"O give thanks to the LORD, for he is good; for his steadfast love endures for ever! Let the redeemed of the LORD say so, whom he has redeemed from trouble and gathered in from the lands, from the east and from the west, from the north and from the south . . . Whoever is wise, let him give heed to these things; let men consider the steadfast love of the LORD."

We give thanks to God for this day. It's a momentous day for Leo and Chee Yin. They represent those redeemed from the East and the West, North and South. From Singapore and North Carolina, God brought them. By His providence, Leo and Chee Yin met, developed a loving relationship, and now wish to nurture their love for a lifetime. God's grace and His plans for us come to fulfillment in such wondrous ways.

A new relationship begins this afternoon, and a new home. As the Bible says, "A man leaves his father and mother and is joined to his wife."

Leo and Chee Yin, please come forward.

Chee Yin and Leo, as you stand here today, you probably wonder what the future will bring for you. There is expectation in your eyes, the anticipation of much joy together. At various times in the early years of marriage to Norma, which is now approaching the thirty-six year mark, I wondered what the future held for us.

Many events lay beyond our control. Actions of other people, so-called acts of God, and near disasters influenced us deeply. But through all the external hardships that were beyond our control, the thing that made the biggest difference with respect to each other — our attitude — was almost completely under our control.

What is the attitude that you should have toward each other? We all know that marriage in our society is supposed to be based on love. But what does it mean to love?

Love, as the Bible describes it, has special meaning — a meaning substantially different from that held by many in our society. This love is not merely an emotion, a tugging in the stomach, or an elevation of mood while in the presence of the other, though it is evident you share these special feelings.

The Bible makes it clear that this love is more than just sexual attraction of a man and a woman. In marriage we are to bring physical joy and satisfaction each to the other. But there is a greater love that helps us do that. The example of our love for the other is seen in God's love for us. God committed Himself to us, He sacrificed Himself for us, and He always forgives.

Love without commitment is often based on nothing stronger than mutual convenience. As such it is subject to dissolution with time and change. But God's love is based on commitment. Thank God, you both already practice this type of commitment.

When you first became believers, you made a commitment to God. As you have lived in faith, you have always known of God's faithfulness to you — that he would never part from you. You knew then as you know now that there is no power on earth that can separate you from God's love. I pray that your commitment to each other will always be just as strong as God's commitment to you.

A second characteristic of God's love is his capacity for self-sacrifice. As Jesus taught us, "Greater love has no one than this, that he lay down his life for his friends" (John 15:13). When he speaks of laying down one's life, he may mean, under certain circumstances, dying to protect another. But the more day-to-day application for your lives is that you must be prepared to overrule your own desires for the welfare of the other.

An infinite capacity for forgiveness is the third characteristic of God's love. He always forgives when we earnestly seek it. Leo and Chee Yin, it is inevitable that you will from time to time wrong each other. But because of your commitment to God's standards, the one of you in the wrong should, when recognizing the mistake, correct it. The other must always be prepared to forgive. Leo, you referred to the fact that three strands together are difficult to break. As the two of you entwine your lives with the Lord you can withstand the threats that destroy lesser relationships.

In summary, the highest and purest form of marital love, indeed, any kind of love, is characterized in the biblical book of 1 Corinthians: "Love is patient, love is kind. It does not envy, it does not boast, it is not proud. It is not rude, it is not self-seeking, it is not easily angered, it keeps no record of wrongs. Love does not delight in evil but rejoices with the truth. It always protects, always trusts, always hopes, always perseveres. Love never fails" (1 Corinthians 13:4-8a).

(Prayer.)

Leo, will you have Chee Yin as your wife, to live together in loving devotion and purity before God? Will you honor her and will you care for her in sickness and in health, in good times and bad? Will you be true to her in mind and body, and will you lead her in righteousness and in the way of the Lord as long as you both live?

(Repeated for Chee Yin)

Please join your right hands, and Leo, would you repeat after me?

I, Leo, take you Chee Yin, to be my wife, and these things I promise you: I will be faithful to you; I will respect, trust, and care for you; I will forgive you as we have been forgiven; and I will try, with you, to better understand ourselves, the world, and God; through the best and worst of what is to come, as long as I live. "Many women have done excellently, but you surpass them all. . . . [A] woman who fears the LORD is to be praised" (Proverbs 31:29, 30, RSV).

Chee Yin, would you repeat after me?

I, Chee Yin, take you Leo, to be my husband, and these things I promise you: I will be faithful to you; I will respect, trust, and care for you; I will forgive you as we have been forgiven, and I will try, with you, to better understand ourselves, the world, and God; through the best and worst of what is to come, as long as I live. "Where you go I will go, and where you lodge I will lodge; your people shall be my people" (Ruth 1:16, RSV), and, God, the Father of our Lord Jesus Christ, will be my God.

Giving of Rings

Leo, place the ring on Chee Yin's finger and repeat after me: "With this ring, I take you as my wife, and we shall walk hand in hand in the path of the Lord."

Chee Yin, place the ring on Leo's finger and repeat after me: "With this ring I take you as my husband, and we shall walk hand in hand in the path of the Lord."

Please rejoin your hands.

Leo and Chee Yin have consented together in marriage before God and before us as witnesses. They have signified this by exchanging vows and the giving of rings. Now by the authority vested in me as a minister of the gospel by the state of California, I pronounce that they are husband and wife.

SAMPLE TAILORED CEREMONY #2

(This ceremony was designed for a couple who had attended our church for a few years. He is of Italian ancestry and owned a small business that specialized in wallpapering. She had moved to Los Angeles from Texas to pursue an acting career.)

Bart and Cindy honor us by allowing us to share this great occasion with them. We are here to celebrate with you, Bart and Cindy, to witness the ceremony, and to let you know of our love and support for you.

We know that you thank God for this moment. We are aware, too, that you are both grateful for your families — for their love and guidance and strength. Your families have done well to bring you to wisdom, maturity, and faith in God.

Who gives Cindy to be married to Bart?

As you stand here today you can't help pondering the future, asking:

What will the years of our marriage bring?

What does the future hold?

How can we make sure that our love will endure and grow?

How can we avoid those painful, devastating wrecks that divide lovers and leave painful, lifelong wounds?

So many couples come to the marriage altar with great expectations of joy, satisfaction, and bliss. Too often that sweet expectation turns to sour anxiety, the satisfaction to frustration, and bliss to a mess. Doors slam. Hopes crush. Only attorneys are happy.

Bart and Cindy, as you stand here today, we are confident that you want your marriage to last, but not just to survive. You have within your grasp, not only the ability to endure the years, but to have great joy. You can build a maturing relationship that creates increasing love each year and awareness you cannot even foresee today.

Jane Austen wrote, "Happiness in marriage is entirely a matter of chance."[1] You have been brought together, not by chance or luck, or stars — but by the great God of the universe who created outer and inner space, innocent little children, and fragrant flowers. He designed your muscles, Bart, and your winning smile. And Cindy, he fashioned that wondrous look of honesty and sincerity in your eyes.

He helped you both develop that marvelous friendship which makes you enjoy each other so much. It is his will that your marriage be happy and mutually satisfying. But in order to know God's will we must follow him. By his grace and by the guidance of your families, you also respect his Word. It is his Word only that can guide you to a future of joy and contentment with each other.

It's tragic, isn't it, that so many people consult *Cosmopolitan* magazine, the *National Enquirer*, and even *Playboy* on how to have a good marriage? They don't recognize that not one of these periodicals now advocates exactly what it did ten to twenty years ago. It is no wonder that people in our society are confused, helpless, and lonely.

Let's look briefly today at the beauty of God's way. Ephesians chapter five, in the New Testament, contains the best formula for marriage ever written.

First, it says, "Submit to one another out of reverence for Christ" (v. 21). People ask, "In a Christian marriage, who is in charge? Wife? Husband? Who?" The answer is, "None of the above." The Lord is. He instructs us, "Submit to one another out of reverence for Christ."

In most marriages, husbands and wives try to gain power over the other. This never works. It is not natural and never brings happiness when one person controls another. How many marriages have you witnessed where the husband vacillates between being a forceful brute and a little boy who has to have his way?

And wives use their methods, too. They often shift between nagging and turning their bodies into refrigerators.

The Lord says, "You could experience so much more joy if you would submit to one another." Couples who do this spend their time bringing delight to the other, and they find increasing satisfaction.

The second thing Ephesians 5 advises is, "Wives, submit to your husbands as to the Lord" (v. 22). Cindy, you do need to submit to Bart — but not because he is muscle-bound and can bark out orders to a bunch of paperhangers. You submit as one whose life is in submission to God. In essence, you are not obeying Bart, but the Lord.

And Bart, the relationship you now maintain with Cindy is the same as you have with your own body. The two of you will now be one flesh. It is unnatural to want to hurt yourself. Bart, from today on, Cindy will be the most beautiful part of you.

As Ephesians 5 reads, "Husbands, love your wives, just as Christ loved the church and gave himself up for her . . . In this same way, husbands ought to love their wives as their own bodies. He who loves his wife loves himself. After all, no one ever hated his own body, but he feeds and cares for it, just as Christ does the church" (vv. 25-29).

Bart, the more you love Cindy and make her smile, the more winsome and lovable she will become. Cindy, the oftener you try to please Bart, the gentler he will be.

God's ways are good and wise. Doing his will assures that in the years and decades ahead, you will experience abundant life, great fulfillment, and increasing love. Challenges and tests you will have, but I'm confident God's love will enable you always.

Some evening, Bart, you will come home tired and weary. That will be the one night in one thousand that Cindy will have burned your favorite spaghetti. It will look like assorted rope ends and used shoelaces. Your feelings of love may be disturbed, but God's love says you have made a forever commitment to Cindy.

Some evening, Cindy when you are especially anxious for Bart to come home, he will call to say he has two more estimates to finish. You will wonder and be upset. Your emotions will say to you, "I'm having trouble loving Bart right now." God's love advises you, "You have made a forever commitment."

There is an old story found in the Jewish Talmud about a couple who had been married for several years but had no children. This distressed the husband; Jewish families hope that one of their sons might be the Messiah. Their conflict led them to seek a divorce, and they consulted their rabbi. He gave approval to the dissolution of the marriage on one condition: they must have a reception to announce it similar to their wedding reception. They agreed and held the party.

During the course of the evening, the husband imbibed too much wine. He said to his wife, "My dear, when you return to your father's house tonight, I want you to choose whatever is most precious to you and take it with you." After that he drank himself into a full stupor.

The wife ordered her servants to pick him up and carry him to the house of her parents. When he awoke the next day, he looked up wondering what had happened. That's when she explained to him, "Last night you told me to choose whatever is most precious to me and bring it here. There is nothing more precious to me than you." I pray that you will always regard each other as that precious.

(Bart's sisters read Scriptures at this time.)

Bart, will you have Cindy as your wedded wife, in righteousness and justice, in steadfast love, and mercy? Will you continue to love and stand by her as Christ did his church? Will Cindy be the sole object of your person in sickness and health, in good times and bad, as long as you both live?

Cindy, will you have Bart as your wedded husband, in righteousness and justice, in steadfast love and mercy? Will you continue to love him as you love the Lord, and stand by him, in sickness and in health, in good times and bad, as long as you both live?

Please join your right hands, and Bart, would you repeat after me?

I, Bart, take you Cindy, as my wedded wife, and these things I promise you: I will stand by you in sickness and in health, in joy and in sorrow; I will respect your needs; I will never forsake you nor leave you; I will love, honor, and cherish you as Christ loves his church; with patience, forgiveness, and godliness, with pure devotion. I will be with you as long as God grants us life.

(This was repeated with necessary changes for Cindy.)

Giving of Rings

(The same for Bart and Cindy.)

   With this ring, I vow to you in humility before the Lord, that you will be my wife, and I shall love you always.

(From this point we used the following order.)

Solo

Prayer

Unity Candle Lighting

Solo

Declaration of Marriage

Kiss

Presentation of Couple

Recessional

NOTES

1. Jane Austen, "Pride and Prejudice." *The Complete Works of Jane Austen* (London: Allan Wingate, 1962), p. 180.

Chapter Twelve

IMPORTANT MISCELLANY

ORDERS OF SERVICE

Unless your denomination requires a certain liturgy, you can choose from a variety of formats. Some ministers follow a certain order as if they were married to it. We need quick divorces from these monographs.

Changing the format is good for several reasons. Different styles of weddings demand it. If your spouse and the members of your congregation have to attend many of your ceremonies, they might appreciate it, too. (Please refer to chapter eleven for the traditional format, and for the order I used in the two tailored ceremonies.)

The following samples are included as possibilities. Other elements or features can be added or deleted by you and the couple. Ask the couple to join right hands during the vows and declarations (pronouncements) of marriage.

Sample "A"

Prelude — music

Processional

Call to Worship — By minister or possibly friend or relative of the couple.

Invitation — Purpose: to invite all of those gathered to witness and give their blessing.

Congregational Response

Solo

Scripture — By minister or by the couple's friend or relative.

Prayer

Congregational Hymn

Vows

Ring Ceremony

Pronouncement of Marriage

Blessing by the Minister

Lord's Prayer

Reading

Homily

Congregational Hymn

Benediction

Kiss

Recessional

Sample "B"
(A brief ceremony; can be used with or without music.)

Prayer

Homily

Acceptance — "Do you, John, take Mary to be your wife . . ."

Ring Ceremony

Declaration of Marriage

Benediction

Blessing

WEDDING TEXTS

Genesis 2:20-25; chapter 24

Ruth 1:16-18

Psalms — The following are rich sources for Calls to Worship and in some cases as wedding texts: Psalms 8; 19; 24; 33:1-9; 67; 81; 89:1, 2, 14-18; 92:1-5; 95:1-7; 96; 98; 100; 105:1-4; 106:1-5; 107:1-3; 108:1-6; 111; 112:1-8; 113; 117; 119:33-40, 89-96, 97-104, 129-136; 136:1-9; 145; 148-150.

Song of Songs — Numerous passages are applicable, especially 2:10-13

Hosea 2:19, 20

1 Corinthians 6:19, 20; 7:1-7; 13

2 Corinthians 3:17, 18; 13:11-14

Ephesians 5:19-33

Philippians 2:1-11; 4:4-9

Colossians 2:6; 3:12-19; 4:2

1 Thessalonians 3:12, 13; 5:16-24

2 Thessalonians 2:16, 17; 3:16

Philemon 4, 5

Hebrews 13:4-6, 15, 16, 20, 21

James 3:17, 18

1 Peter 3:1-7

1 John 2:28; 4:4-19

2 John 6

Jude 2, 24, 25

Revelation 21:1, 2

WEDDING VOWS

Paraphrased from Proverbs by Thomas Weber

May my conduct always be such that you never lose trust in me.

May you never lack any good thing.

I will try to do you good and not harm all the days of your life.

My hands will always be willing to work for you.

Any time of the day or night, I will rise to care for you.

I will provide for our household and not be lazy.

I will be considerate and plan for our future.

I will try to be optimistic and a light for you in the world.

I will try to see things as you see them.

May we never fear disaster and always be prepared.

May I never do anything to shame you, and may I always speak with wisdom and kindness; and may you always be able to speak well of me.

I will clothe myself with strength and dignity.

Health and strength will be my belt; and may I joyfully go into old age with you.

May our actions towards each other always speak louder than our words.

May we always respect and love the Lord.

SAMPLE APPLICATIONS

Application to Have Minister Perform

Wedding of: _____ Date of Application _____

_____ Time of Wedding _____

_____ Location of Wedding _____

Full name of bride _____ Phone _____

Present Address_____

               (Street)   (City)   (State) (Zip)

Residence after marriage_____

Employed by _____ Occupation _____

Age _____ Place of Birth _____

Have you had a previous marriage? __ How did it end? _____

If by divorce, when? ____ Have you had counseling? _____

By whom? _____

Church Membership _____ Attend where? _____

How long have you known the person you plan to marry? ___

What factors lead you to believe you will have a happy marriage? _____

_____

_____

Do you have any physical conditions that might impair your relationship? _____

_____

Have you discussed this with a physician? _____

Have you discussed this with your fiancé?* _____

*Spelling for a man engaged to be married, fiancée for a woman.

Father's name _____ Mother's maiden name _____

How would you rate the married life of your parents on a scale of one to ten? _____

(One = very unsatisfactory, ten = very successful)

Using the same scale, how would you rate their attitude toward your marriage?

Father _____ Mother _____ Stepparent, if applicable _____

(Repeat the above information for the groom applicant)

(For both)

Are you willing to have x number of counseling sessions prior to your marriage?____ Days of the week and times that you can meet with the counselor _____
                       (Days)   (Times)

WEDDING INFORMATION

Date _____ Time _____

Groom	**Bride**
Name _____	Name _____
Address _____	Address _____
_____	_____
Home Phone ( ) _____	Home Phone ( ) _____
Work Phone ( ) _____	Work Phone ( ) _____
Best Man _____	Maid/Matron of Honor _____
His Phone ( ) _____	Her Phone ( ) _____
Groomsmen _____	Bridesmaids _____
_____	_____
_____	_____
_____	_____
Ushers _____	Flower Girl _____
_____	Ring Bearer _____
_____	Father _____
Father _____	Mother _____
Mother _____	Will someone other than the father present the bride? ___
Names of grandparents who will be participating in ceremony _____	Name of Presenter _____
_____	Name of grandparents who will participate _____
Photographer _____	_____
His Phone ( ) _____	Florist _____
Organist _____	Aisle Runner: Yes ___ No ___

Name(s) of Soloist _____

Names of Other Participants,
e.g., Readers or Musicians __

_____

_____

NOTES AND COMMENTS:

Unity Candle Service:

Yes ___ No___

Reception time _____

Location _____

Rehearsal Date & Time _____

***Minister must have your
marriage license prior to
rehearsal.**

Address after marriage _____

_____

NOTE: In shrinking the forms to fit this book size, some of the lines
are shorter than needed to write on. When you make your own form
(on 8½ × 11 paper), be sure to allow enough room to fill in.

Church Building Use Application

(Subject to conditions on attached sheet.)

Wedding Date _____ Hour _____

Rehearsal Date _____ Hour _____

Minister _____ Phone (   ) _____

Organist _____ Phone, if other than church organist _____

Florist and Phone # _____

Caterer and Phone # _____

Groom _____ Phone _____

Address _____

Member of What Church _____

Bride _____ Phone _____

Address _____

Member of What Church _____

We have read the conditions on the attached sheet of this application and agree to abide by them if we are permitted use of the church facilities. We shall make every effort to ensure that our guests will do likewise.

_____   _____
Applicant Bride   Date   Applicant Groom   Date

Please return to church office by _____
                                              Date

Approved by _____
                                              Date

Conditions: Please Read Carefully

(I suggest the use of separate forms for members and non-members as donations, fees, and policies may vary.)

Schedule of Charges or Suggested Donations:

For Use of Church Sanctuary .... $xxxxx

For Use of Church Chapel .... $xxxxx

Additional for Rehearsal .... $xxxxx

Use of Lounge or Dining Facilities for Reception ... $xxxxx

Sound Technician .... $xxxxx

Church Hostess .... $xxxxx

Church Organist or Musicians .... $xxxxx

Extra Janitorial Services .... $xxxxx

Policy Statement

The following items should be considered:

1) List days and hours of the week the facilities are unavailable.

2) Policy concerning food and drink in other than dining area.

3) Smoking and liquor policy.

4) Policy on the use of rice, confetti, and birdseed.

5) State times when building will be open for floral deliveries and to pick up baskets, candelabra, etc., following the service.

6) Payment or deposit for facilities should be made with submission of application.

CONFIGURATIONS

Configurations for processionals, recessionals, and for the ceremonies follow for your convenience. These orders are not etched in stone and probably shouldn't be ingrained in the floor of your church building either. Orders of service and configurations are traditions that can be changed by the bride, the groom, and you. The custom of having the groom stand on the right came about from the need of grooms in ancient times to fend off rival suitors for the brides. Grooms needed right arms free for ready access to their swords. Their most trusted friends stood at their right to assist them. Presumably society won't revert to those "good old days."

After scores of weddings in California, I had a first at a wedding at which I officiated in Iowa. The groom asked if his elder sister could serve as "best man." There was no reason that she couldn't except for centuries of tradition. She wore a dignified black dress and performed all her duties capably.

Sample configurations include:
   (1) A typical Protestant ceremony;
   (2) An alternate Protestant ceremony;
   (3) A typical Jewish ceremony.
Each set includes the proper order for the processional, the recessional, and a diagram showing where members of the wedding party stand during the ceremony.

Why have I shown configurations for a Jewish ceremony? In Jewish weddings, there is a strong emphasis on families. Parents and grandparents usually accompany both the bride and the groom down the aisle. At times they also serve as standing witnesses. I would love to see this emphasis on families and respect for elders in Christian weddings.

TYPICAL PROTESTANT PROCESSIONAL

Minister

Father & bride

Groom   Best man

Groomsmen-ushers

Bridesmaids

Maid (matron) of honor

Ring bearer

Flower girl

TYPICAL PROTESTANT CEREMONY

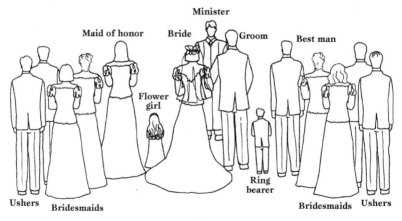

Minister

Maid of honor   Bride   Groom   Best man

Flower
girl

Ushers   Ushers
      Bridesmaids   Bridesmaids

Ring
bearer

TYPICAL PROTESTANT RECESSIONAL

ALTERNATE PROTESTANT PROCESSIONAL

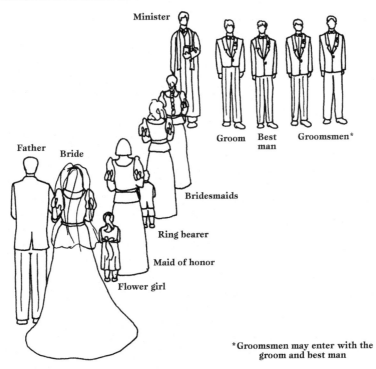

*Groomsmen may enter with the groom and best man

ALTERNATE PROTESTANT CEREMONY

ALTERNATE PROTESTANT RECESSIONAL

TYPICAL JEWISH PROCESSIONAL

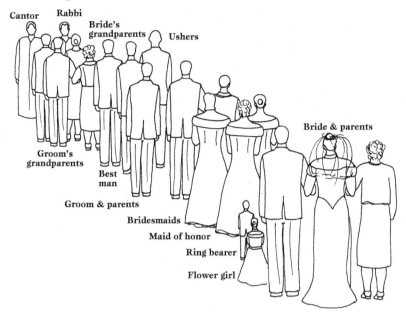

Cantor
Rabbi
Bride's grandparents
Ushers
Groom's grandparents
Best man
Groom & parents
Bridesmaids
Maid of honor
Ring bearer
Flower girl
Bride & parents

TYPICAL JEWISH CEREMONY

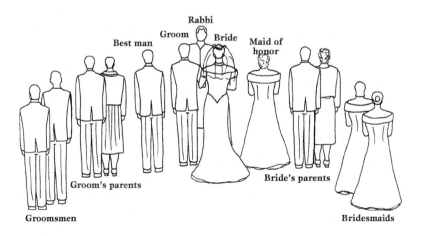

Rabbi
Groom
Bride
Best man
Maid of honor
Groom's parents
Bride's parents
Groomsmen
Bridesmaids

TYPICAL JEWISH RECESSIONAL

Cantor · Rabbi

Ring bearer · Flower girl · Bridesmaids

Ushers

Best man

Maid of honor

Groom's grandparents
Bride's grandparents

Groom's parents
Bride's parents

Bride & groom

Selected Reading List

Abingdon Marriage Manual, revised edition by P. Biddle, Abingdon, Nashville, 1987.

Baker's Wedding Handbook: A Comprehensive Guide to Eleven Denominational Traditions by Paul Engle, Baker Book House, Grand Rapids, MI, 1994.

Getting Ready for Marriage Workbook by Hardin and Sloan, Thomas Nelson, Nashville, 1992.

Intimate Encounters by Ferguson and Thurman, Thomas Nelson, Nashville, 1994.

Leadership Handbooks of Practical Theology, Volume One, Word & Worship, General Editor, James D. Berkley, Baker Book House, Grand Rapids, MI, 1992, pp. 413-459.

Love Life for Every Married Couple by Ed Wheat, M.D., Zondervan, Grand Rapids, MI, 1980.

The Marriage Builder by Dr. Larry Crabb, Zondervan, Grand Rapids, MI, 1992.

The New Westminster Dictionary of Liturgy and Worship, J.G. Davies, editor, Westminster, Philadelphia, 1986.

The Spirit-Controlled Temperament by Tim LaHaye, Tyndale House, Wheaton, IL, 1984.

When Victims Marry by Don and Jan Frank, Thomas Nelson, Nashville, 1993.

Worship Is a Verb by Robert E. Webber, Word Books, Waco, TX, 1985.

For the latest in wedding customs, consult *Bride's Magazine*, published six times a year by Condé Nast Publications, New York. It's probably available in your local library.